IN THE MIDST OF THE CITY

THE GOSPEL AND GOD'S POLITICS

IN THE
MIDST
OF THE
CITY

THE GOSPEL AND GOD'S POLITICS

BARKLEY S. THOMPSON
Foreword by the Honorable Linnet Deily

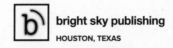

bright sky publishing

HOUSTON, TEXAS

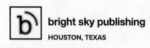 **bright sky publishing**
HOUSTON, TEXAS

2365 Rice Blvd., Suite 202
Houston, Texas 77005

ISBN: 978-1-942945-69-7

10 9 8 7 6 5 4 3 2 1

Library of Congress Cataloging-in-Publication Data on file with the publisher.

Editorial Director: Lucy Herring Chambers
Designer: Marla Y. Garcia

Printed in Canada by Friesens

"I Am Watching, Says the Lord" first appeared in the Belief section of the
Houston Chronicle.

For the people of Christ Church Cathedral,
Houston, Texas, who faithfully proclaim
God in the midst of the city.

God is in the midst of the city:
it shall not be moved;
God will help it when the morning dawns.

PSALM 46:5

Table of Contents

Foreword

IN 2012, following the retirement of Christ Church Cathedral's dean, the Cathedral search committee began working to identify and call the new dean. Several months into the process, from within the Diocese of Texas and other parts of the Episcopal world, we began receiving recommendations for Barkley Thompson. Reverend Thompson then served as the rector of St. John's Episcopal Church in Roanoke, Virginia, so four of us from the search committee made a trip there to hear him preach, visit with him about the Cathedral, and explore his candidacy to become "our" dean.

Over that weekend, we heard Rev. Thompson preach at four separate services, and we also spent more than five hours interviewing him exhaustively on a wide range of topics. We conducted two additional hours of interviews when he and his wife, Jill, visited Houston later in the year. At one point in this process, we began to focus our conversation on practical questions about Thompson's preaching: What was his style? How often did he preach? How did he prepare? Did he preach political sermons? Mind you, we were still in the midst of "getting-to-know-you," without any deep foundation of awareness and trust, but Thompson understood the critical nature of this last question on preaching politics and paused to answer in some depth.

He explained to us that he tried to preach the Gospel faithfully in his sermons and that sometimes that message reflected on a particular issue of the day. At other times, the events themselves seemed to require a Gospel response, and he used the example of the aftermath of 9/11 as such an event. Thompson was clear in distinguishing that his preaching was never partisan; but, rather, was intended to be instructive of God's call to us as Christians.

Subsequent to his arrival at Christ Church, we also witnessed this connection between the Gospel and the external world through a series of discussions that Dean Thompson calls "Faith and Society." He had grappled in his ministry with the conundrum of how to engage parishioners in conversation about significant societal issues without simultaneously starting a conflagration in the congregation. While in Roanoke, he had participated in such a discussion led by the Aspen Institute and decided to adopt their ground rules in hopes of conducting such a dialogue, and he brought that successful practice to Houston. Each participant—and there were around thirty of us in the group—had to commit to attend regularly for a season, exchange views without condemnation of the others' perspectives, and read all the suggested background materials before the meetings.

Over the intervening years the Faith and Society seminar has discussed almost every hot-button issue in contemporary society—abortion, same-sex marriage, gun control, poverty, war, immigration, to name a few. And we have always conducted the sessions in an open and frank style without any discord—disagreement, yes, but not discord. Before each meeting Dean Thompson provided the group with six to eight readings on the topic. He always started the readings with pertinent selections from the Bible and then included additional readings that presented either side of the session's difficult issue. While our covenant for civility certainly influenced the positive nature of the dialogue, grounding each discussion in the Gospel—not for proof points, but for context and illumination—again reinforced the Gospel-grounded nature of his ministry.

Revisiting the sermons and essays included in this manuscript, I'm reminded frequently of the prophetic nature of Dean Thompson's words. He is not calling us to accept specific answers on issues, but rather, to live our lives and choose our political stances as people of God, firmly grounded in God's call. As you read this book, I encourage you to begin each section by reflecting first on God's vision for the world—and then to focus on the event or issue highlighted in the chapter. Please see for yourself if this perspective deepens your own awareness of God's message to us.

The Honorable Linnet Deily
Former United States Ambassador to the World Trade Organization

IN THE MIDST OF THE CITY

Introduction
GOD'S POLITICS

ON PALM SUNDAY, Christians across the globe partici-
pate in reenactments of Jesus's triumphal procession into
Jerusalem. They wave palm fronds and sing "Hosannah!"
enjoying the color and pageantry of the once-a-year event.
I daresay that most Christians would be surprised—
shocked, even—to learn that their participation in the
Palm Sunday liturgy is a political act.

Imagine yourself in Jerusalem on the first Palm Sunday,
on or near the year A.D. 30[1]. In the preceding days the
population of Jerusalem has swelled with all the Jews who
have come to celebrate the Passover festival. In Jerusalem,
Passover often brings unrest, as the subjugated Jews
gather in critical mass and compare stories of Roman oppression and hopes of Jewish liberation. To squelch any
rabble-rousing, on the first day of the week the Roman
governor of Judea, Pontius Pilate, processes into Jerusalem
from his western coastal capital, Caesarea Maritima, at

the head of a column of Roman soldiers in full military parade. Hoisting the golden eagle of Rome and embodying the empire's power and grandeur, Pilate makes a point that cannot be missed by the Jews packed into Rome for Passover. Though these Jews are in the city to celebrate the God who once delivered them from Pharaoh's bondage, such lightning will not strike twice. Rome's imperial power is unassailable. Caesar is the only god who matters.

In conscious contrast to Pontius Pilate's procession from the west, Jesus makes his own plans to enter the city from the Mount of Olives in the east. Jesus understands himself to stand in the tradition of the prophets, and he knows that the prophet Zechariah said a king will appear in Jerusalem "humble, and riding on a colt, the foal of a donkey." And what will this king accomplish? Zechariah says, "He will cut off the chariot from Ephraim and the war-horse from Jerusalem; and the battle bow shall be cut off, and he shall command peace to the nations."[2]

Jesus orchestrates his entry into Jerusalem exactly to fit Zechariah's prophecy. Jesus enters the city from the east at the beginning of Passover week as a deliberate and impossible-to-miss counter to Pontius Pilate's concurrent procession from the west. For all those Jews gathered in Jerusalem, Jesus's procession provides an alternative narrative to Pilate's. Through his prophetic action Jesus proclaims that Rome's domination is not the only, or the ultimate, reality. Even under Rome's oppressive and watchful eye, *God enters into the midst of the city*. And like rivulets of water through stone, God's very presence eventually will break open the old order in favor of something new.

Pilate's procession symbolizes the power of war. Jesus's procession symbolizes the power of peace. Pilate's procession stands for the empire of Caesar. Jesus's procession stands for the kingdom of God. Each time Christians reenact the Palm Sunday liturgy, we are siding with the latter over the former. We are standing with Jesus against the powers of the world. We are engaging in a political act.

Jesus was political. The Gospel is a political text. I am repeatedly amazed at the number of people who say to me, "I want politics kept out of the church." Such exclusion is impossible, if we are faithful. As mentioned above, Jesus self-consciously placed himself in the prophetic tradition, and his politics finds its source in the Old Testament prophetic witness.

Christian theologian and ethicist John Howard Yoder says, "No 'bridge' or 'translation' is needed to make the Bible a book about politics. The new order, the new humanity, does not replace or destroy the old, but that does not make the new order apolitical. Its very existence is subversive at the points where the old order is repressive, and creative where the old is without vision. The transcendence of the new [order] consists not in its escaping the realm where the old order rules, but in its subverting and transforming that realm. It does that by virtue of its being an alternative story."[3]

What is politics? It is commentary and action that affect the *polis* and the *polis's civitas*: the citizens for whom the *polis* is home. God claims the whole world as the *polis* in which the Gospel's alternative story is to become reality. God claims the whole creation as God's kingdom. And God's vision is not an ethereal, spiritual one.

When Jesus says in Luke 6, "Blessed are the poor," he does not refer to upper middle-class people battling existential emptiness. Jesus refers literally to those who subsist on the very margins of society. When in Matthew 25 Jesus condemns those who withhold care from the hungry, the sick, and the imprisoned and embraces those who love them, he is speaking concretely. When Jesus appropriates the words of the prophet Isaiah as his own in Luke 4:17-21, proclaiming, "The Spirit of the Lord is upon me, because he has anointed me to proclaim good news to the poor. He has sent me to proclaim freedom for the prisoners and recovery of sight for the blind, to set the oppressed free, to proclaim the year of the Lord's favor," he is not speaking in metaphor.

The politics of God is *commentary and action that proclaim the advent of God's kingdom in the world.* It is a narrative of liberation, of peace, of reconciliation, and of grace. It is what Jesus himself proclaims through his Palm Sunday procession. Indeed, it is what Jesus proclaimed from the very beginning of his ministry. And its ultimate triumph is what God ensured through the Resurrection of Jesus on Easter.

For Christians—disciples of Jesus who choose to march in Jesus's alternative Palm Sunday procession rather than Pontius Pilate's—leaving God's politics out of the church is not an option. Just as Jesus's procession subversively declares that God enters into the midst of the city, we must acknowledge that God enters into the midst of every aspect of our lives, public as well as private. It is the central role of the church to be the Body of Christ: to be Christ's voice, hands, and feet; to enact the commentary and action that proclaim the advent of God's kingdom in the world. Without politics, there is no church.

The Gospel, however, is not partisan. My words do not intend to imply that I endorse the political agenda of one secular political party or another or, worse yet, that Jesus endorses the political agenda of one political party or another. Jesus does not (nor do I).

Secular politics differs from God's politics. As Bishop Andy Doyle points out in his book *The Jesus Heist*, both conservative and progressive secular politics are rooted in the humanism of the Enlightenment. Bishop Doyle says, "One of these positions revolves around the self and the preservation of the self. It is a humanism focused on the individual over against the other...This is a kind of rugged 'pull yourself up by your bootstraps' individualism...The second...is rooted in an appreciation for community. Instead of the self as the organizing motif, communal well-being becomes the organizing motif...This orientation always focuses on the individual in relationship to the 'other.'"[4]

Any modern person can immediately see value in both political positions—preserving the integrity and rights of the individual and preserving the bonds of community—but in each case this value is limited because, as Bishop Doyle points out, "Both strands of humanism tend toward power play."[5] Ultimately, secular politics—both conservative and progressive—is about power: who wields it, and who makes decisions that are binding upon others. At the center of all secular politics is *us*, and in any endeavor that puts human actors in the center, those actors will begin to function in favor of preserving their power over and against others. Those actors will also coopt any means to accomplish their ends, including the Gospel.

To so coopt the Gospel is tantalizingly easy. I see it frequently, from both ends of the political spectrum. Both conservative and progressive Christians will espouse a deeply-held political view and then plumb the Gospel for support of that view. It should be noted: I have never encountered anyone who failed in this attempt! Taken out of context, wrenched from the sweep and trajectory of God's alternative narrative for the world, human ingenuity will always find a way to pervert the Gospel for its own purposes. And yet, to do so is always an error in discernment.

Bishop Doyle goes on to say, "Human flourishing, regardless of being oriented around the individual or society, is not the end purpose of God in Christ Jesus...Doing things for each other out of our pure sense of shared humanity and our moral devices are not enough to overcome the self-centeredness that plagues our various humanisms. The purpose of God in Christ Jesus is to gather all of humanity into God's self."[6]

The Gospel does not grow from roots in the Enlightenment. It does not put God in service to human ends, no matter how noble those ends may purport—or truly believe themselves—to be. Rather, the Gospel reveals that true human flourishing begins when we recognize that our lives are grounded in God and when we set aside our own ends in favor of God's alternative vision for us and for the world.

Simply put: The Gospel is not partisan, and God is neither a conservative nor a progressive. As Christians, we must not begin with our secular political beliefs, convictions, and commitments and then use the Gospel to prop them up. Rather, we must begin with the Gospel and allow the Gospel to shape our politics whole-cloth. Christians are not, ultimately speaking, conservatives or progressives. Ultimately, Christians are disciples of Jesus. Our only politics must be God's politics. Our commentary and actions must only be those birthed by the Gospel of Jesus.

How do we do this, practically speaking? How do we gauge the ways in which God's politics bears upon the concrete and the contextual in our day-to-day world? How do we discern how to speak and act? The great theologian Karl Barth famously said, "Take your Bible and take your newspaper, and read both. But interpret newspapers from your Bible," never the other way around.[7]

It is a requirement of fidelity to the Gospel that we study the Gospel, attentively and deeply. Merely hearing passages read from the Lectionary on the occasional Sunday morning does not disciples make. The only effective hedge against coopting the Gospel for secular political ends is to know the Gospel intimately in its sweep and trajectory. The Gospel must become both companion and signpost that guide us moment-by-moment as we navigate life. The Gospel must be the lodestone that draws us continually back to Jesus's Palm Sunday procession whenever the secular world entices us with Pilate's pomp and worldly power.

It is also a requirement of fidelity to the Gospel that Christians be informed about the world. We must, as Karl Barth counsels, read the newspaper in addition to the Bible. However, and as I amplify in the sermons "Skimming the Headlines" and "The Mystic Chords" included in this volume, this means resisting the urge only to graze superficialities or only to imbibe information from sources with which the reader already agrees. We must read broadly and deeply, question honestly and carefully, and then discern our commentary and action by interpreting the news of the world and crafting our response to it through the lens of the Gospel.

This is what I seek to do, with God's help, in my preaching and writing. The sermons and essays that follow are responses to Karl Barth's dictum. Each of the sermons in the first section of this volume was written in and for the community of Christ Church Cathedral in Houston, Texas—a place and a people who embody the Body of Christ and live God's politics in ways that inspire me and nourish my hope. Each sermon responds to an actual event in the world, ranging from acts of terror and natural disasters to political folly and national elections.

The second section of the book takes a step back and asks, from the standpoint of Independence Day, what it means, in light of the Gospel, to be a Christian and an American. It won't surprise the reader that the sequence of these identifiers is not incidental. Foundationally, we are always Christian first and American second.

Finally, section three presents essays that were first published on my blog, *God in the Midst of the City*, in the *Houston Chronicle*, or both. These essays represent my personal process of discernment, as I seek in faith to begin with God's alternative vision for the world and let it inform my way of being, rather than beginning with a secular political position and misusing the Gospel to undergird it.

The piece "I Own Guns, and I Believe in Gun Control" appeared in both my blog and the *Houston Chronicle* and was also circulated by the Brady Center to Prevent Gun Violence. It is the only piece I've ever written that elicited death threats. "Of Orlando and the Virtue of Embrace" was my response to the LGBTQ community after the horrific Pulse nightclub shooting. I wrote "'I Am Watching,' Says the Lord" as an op-ed in the *Houston Chronicle*, which was co-signed by several fellow local clerics. "On Civil War Monuments" first appeared on my blog and eventually found its way to the Duke University presidential commission studying the presence of Civil War monuments on the Duke campus.

God abides not only, or even primarily, in our church buildings. God is about in the world. God is in the midst of the city. God is vitally concerned with the *polis*, and God calls the disciples of Jesus to be the vanguard of God's kingdom in the world, to embody the alternative narrative of liberation, peace, reconciliation, and grace that human beings encounter when we remove ourselves and our power plays from the center and instead find our center in God. The decision to march in the procession of Jesus or the procession of Pontius Pilate is always before us. As the pieces in this volume challenge us to do, we are called, in other words, to live God's politics.

Breaking News

1

Look for the Helpers

REVELATION 7:9-17

SUNDAY, APRIL 21, 2013

ON APRIL 15, 2013, two pressure cooker bombs exploded near the finish line of the Boston Marathon, killing three people and wounding more than one hundred. The bombers were brothers Dzokhar and Tamerlan Tsarnaev, who evaded authorities for three days thereafter, killing a policeman and wounding two others, one of whom also later died. Tamerlan Tsarnaev was killed in a police shootout on April 18. Dzhokhar was captured on April 19.

On the video, the first thing one notices is the brightness of the sky. It is a near perfect day. The sun is shining, and the temperature reaches a crisp and refreshing fifty-four degrees. On this same date last year, the thermometer soared into the nineties, overflowing the medical tent with heat-related illnesses. But not this day. This day is a near perfect day.

The second thing one notices is the discrepancy between the few people running in the road and the multitudes lining the sidewalks. Two-thirds of the runners have already finished their race. Those who remain on the road are the determined, the dogged, the people for whom merely entering and finishing this historic route has been a lifelong dream. One is a seventy-eight-year-old man. Even so, the crowd lining the sidewalk has not thinned. They cheer for these final runners as though they are about to win the Olympics.

The third thing one notices is the array of colorful flags waving in the breeze. From the vantage point of the video, one can count thirty national flags, and more extend beyond the line of sight. The flags represent the runners, the spectators, and all of us who look to events like the Boston Marathon for reminders that occasionally the best impulses of humanity emerge. Runners from across the globe gather not only to compete but also simply to share in this iconic experience. Kenyan standing next to Canadian standing alongside American all shout encouragement for the runners and, really, for the whole human family.

It is an earthly approximation of the heavenly vision in Revelation. St. John the Divine tells us, "After this I looked, and there was a great multitude that no one could count, from every nation, from all tribes and peoples and languages, standing before the throne and before the Lamb..."

Those colorful, international flags are waving in the breeze when the bomb explodes. The force of the blast shreds some of them. The seventy-eight-year-old runner crumbles to the ground. Three people are killed immediately. Hundreds are wounded, many gruesomely. Instantly, the world is shattered. Essayist Patricia Adams Farmer reminds us, "If we live long enough and deep enough, at some point in life, we will experience a quaking and breaking of everything we considered solid and sure."[1]

True indeed. But must it happen so often? I have only recently moved to Houston from Roanoke, Virginia, just down the road from Blacksburg, where the Virginia Tech massacre is still so recent its pain is searing for many. I have just returned from the Conference of North American Cathedral Deans, where the dean in Oklahoma City tells me his parishioners are still, so many years later, reminded daily of the grotesque attack on the Alfred P. Murrah Federal Building that killed one hundred sixty-eight people including nineteen children. And there is Columbine. And there is Sandy Hook. And there is 9/11.

Add to such newsworthy events all the mundane tragedies of our lives—the illnesses, the accidents, the failures, the injuries we do to one another—and it seems that Patricia Adams Farmer is wrong in one respect: We don't really have to live very long or very deep to experience the quaking and breaking of everything.

As news of the bombings in Boston quickly spread, countless people succumbed to such reflections. I did, too. But then I watched *The Boston Globe*'s video of the explosion a second time. When I did, something new stood out in stark relief to the carnage. I have no idea who held the video camera. I don't know his name, his occupation, or what he had for breakfast that morning. What I do know is that exactly two seconds after the first bomb detonates— two seconds—the cameraman breaks into a run. But he does not run away; he does not run for cover. He runs toward the blast; he runs into the smoke. And as his video camera jostles and shakes, I can see all around him the multitude of people doing exactly the same thing. They run toward those shredded flags representing so many peoples and nations. They run into the chaos.

The late Fred Rogers, the beloved children's television host, shared this: "When I was a boy and I would see scary things in the news, my mother would say to me, 'Look for the helpers. You will always find people who are helping.' To this day, especially in times of disaster, I remember my mother's words, and I am always comforted by realizing that there are still so many helpers—so many caring people in this world."[2]

With Fred Roger's words echoing in my mind, I look back upon all those tragedies, the headliners and the personal ones, and I see the helpers. I see the stranger who brought an exhausted father a cup of coffee in a surgical waiting room just yesterday morning. I see the group of people who tackled the knife-wielding assailant at Lone Star College last week so he couldn't harm anyone else. I see the clients of our homeless center, The Beacon— homeless men and women—who rushed into the busy street to protect a Cathedral parishioner who was clipped by a hit-and-run driver three weeks ago. And I see—until my dying day I will see—the hundreds of emergency responders who rushed into the hell of two smoking towers in lower Manhattan a decade ago.

In Revelation, St. John asks his angelic guide who the multitude might be, streaming to and surrounding the throne of God. The guide says, "These are they who have come out of the great ordeal; they have washed their robes and made them white in the blood of the Lamb. For this reason they are before the throne of God."

It turns out the scene at the Boston Marathon truly was an earthly vision of that heavenly scene. Those who streamed into that great ordeal represented a multitude of peoples and nations. Some of them undoubtedly pray to God-in-Christ; some pray to God by other names; some likely don't know what to call God at all. Regardless, it wasn't the smoke that attracted them; it wasn't chaos for chaos' sake. They ran into the ordeal, and they washed their robes in the blood of the wounded, because they were attracted by love, instinctively and overpoweringly. And God is love.

On his blog, Pastor Steve Garnaas-Holmes responded to the Boston Marathon bombing by saying, "It's not easy. Love is not quick, and does not produce immediate results. It's a marathon. It takes dedication and training and a lot of commitment. It's not for the faint-hearted...Love takes guts. It takes faith, confidence that a greater love is at work even when we cannot see it. And it takes patience, like a marathon—the willingness to go the distance, to keep at it when your body cries, 'Quit!,' when your mind thinks of better things to do, when pain and weariness make you want to give up—it takes guts to keep going anyway... To share in the world's pain and sadness, and still keep up hope and love—that is the world's oldest marathon. The good news is that we do not run alone. Nor do we run on our own energy: we are moved by the desire of God for the healing of the world."[3]

The final promise of Revelation today is that, in God's good time, the ordeal will end. "[We] will hunger no more, and thirst no more…for the Lamb at the center of the throne will be [our] shepherd, and he will guide [us] to springs of the water of life. And God will wipe away every tear from [our] eyes."

I believe that promise. But we live in the meantime, in which two misguided young men possessed by anger and fear detonate bombs and destroy near perfect days. The author Frederick Buechner, never one to sugar-coat, says, "Here is the world. Beautiful and terrible things will happen. Don't be afraid."[4]

We need not fear, even in the meantime, because God is love, and God has disciples who will always stream into the chaos on behalf of that love. Look for the helpers. There are so many of them.

2

Paris, Syria, and Christ the King

JOHN 18:33-37, 2 SAMUEL 23:1-7

NOVEMBER 22, 2015

ON NOVEMBER 13, 2015, the Islamic State in Syria and al-Sham (ISIS) perpetrated a coordinated terrorist attack in Paris, including suicide bombers outside the Stade de France football stadium, shooters at several cafes, and shooters at the Bataclan Theatre during a crowded rock concert. In all, one hundred thirty people were killed. Concurrently, the Syrian Civil War raged, and more than four million Syrians had fled their country seeking refugee status elsewhere. It was the largest mass migration of people since World War II.

Recently, I visited the National Center for Civil and Human Rights in Atlanta. Interspersed among the timelines and photographs, the center includes vintage television sets that loop old broadcast interviews with George Wallace, Bull Connor, and others, all of whom say, in the vernacular of the era, that "the Negro" is an inherent threat to the white man and must be segregated from white society. The voices imply violence and fan fear. As one moves through the exhibit, the sounds of these voices are never quite silenced. They haunt; they distract; they needle their way into consciousness.

2 Samuel today reveals to us the final, benedictory words of King David, the ideal king of Israel. They reveal one side of the great king, the spiritual side that cleaves to God and serves as God's oracle. At the beginning of the Bible's next book, however, we receive the very last image of David, and it reminds us of David's other, worldly side. In 1 Kings we read that "King David was old and advanced in years, and although they covered him with clothes, he could not get warm."[1] That's a starkly realistic and even pitiful image. The man who once slew Goliath, who defeated armies, who built Jerusalem, is now so diminished that he can't even beat back the cold.

And for those who know the story of David in full, we are reminded at this point that this ideal king is also an entirely and sometimes viciously human one. He is the potentate who forced himself upon Bathsheba, who intentionally sent her husband Uriah to his death, who went to any length to accomplish whatever he desired. We remember the David who, in order to get what he wanted, knew when to stoke his nation's patriotism and when to fan his people's fears, who sometimes entered into alliances with other kings, availing himself of their protection, and at other times vilified his neighbors as something less than his own people.

But now this king, who has for so long molded the world into his image, embodies the image of one who is diminished, and in pain, and cold, and about to die. Because that is what happens to the kings of this world, all of them, whether they wear crowns, or suits, or desert tunics; whether they sit in Jerusalem or Washington, DC, Austin or Fallujah; whether they call themselves Highness or President, Governor or Caliph. They, like all of us, are but dust, and to dust they will return. And the worlds they build? The petty empires? Scripture has something to say about those, too. The author of Ecclesiastes begins his wise treatise by saying, "Vanity of vanities, all is vanity."

Why does this matter on this particular day? Because today is the last Sunday of our liturgical year. Next Sunday we enter Advent, in which we assume the posture of expectation and anticipation. But today we pause to assume a different posture, one of kneeling subjects, and the king to whom we kneel is not David or any earthly king, whatever title he may bear. Today is the day we declare Christ the King.

In John's Gospel today, another of those worldly kings, the Roman prefect Pontius Pilate, questions Jesus. On the face of it, in this encounter Pilate has absolute power, and Jesus has absolutely none. Pilate explains that others are calling Jesus king. Pilate knows what kings do. He knows how kings act. And so he asks Jesus, "What have you done? What are the tell-tale signs of your kingship? How will you fight back, or where will you circle the wagons?"

Jesus's response, refracted through the Gospel he has preached and lived, is to say, "My kingdom is not one among others. My kingdom operates by completely different rules—rules not of this world—rules that don't derive from your binary calculus of winners and losers, of us against them, of might makes right, of power preying on the powerless."

Pilate shrugs and scoffs, and he sends Jesus off to the cross. That's what kings with worldly power do to the powerless. And Jesus dies. But his death is not like the irrevocable diminishment and decay of David, or of Pilate for that matter, or of all worldly kings.

Jesus's death is a testament to love, which will not raise a hand in violence and will not exclude anyone from its embrace. Jesus's death is revealed to be the first step in resurrection. While all other kings ultimately lie irrelevant in the grave, Jesus the King lives eternally on; and his reign increases whenever and wherever souls serve Christ the King by resisting those haunting voices that needle our ears, fomenting violence and fanning fear and, instead, choose to act not according to the ways of the world, but according to the law of love.

On November 13, 2015, the voice of a worldly, self-declared king named Abu Bakr al-Baghdadi fanned his ISIS followers to launch coordinated terrorist attacks throughout Paris, killing one hundred thirty people and wounding hundreds more. It was not, by the way, the only day of terror that week. The day before, ISIS had killed forty-three people in Beirut.

What rules of worldly kingdoms would lead to such attacks? To understand this, we must back up and acknowledge what happened in the twelve months prior to that week. As the result of civil war, compounded by the horrific brutality of ISIS toward anyone who won't subscribe to its specific version of Islam, Syria is emptying.

Think about that. It is unprecedented in modern history, and it represents the largest mass migration of people since World War II.[2] Hundreds of thousands of refugees, fleeing for their lives and the lives of their families, have reached Europe, where nations including France and Germany have opened their doors and granted sanctuary. Women, children, and families have been extended grace, care, and safety. Make no mistake: Where this has happened, we have seen a striking and hopeful geo-political glimpse of God's kingdom on earth.

And that, as Paul Goldsmith has astutely observed, is exactly why these attacks in Paris occurred.[3] Al-Baghdadi has stated publicly that ISIS wishes to eliminate any sense that it is possible for Muslims and non-Muslims to co-exist, because where they do co-exist, the dualistic ISIS worldview of black and white, believer and infidel, breaks down. The very intention behind the ISIS attacks was to sow seeds of fear, to pit the West against those seeking safety for their families. As Paul Goldsmith says, "ISIS realized they had to do something to stop us taking in refugees. They had to do something to remind us that Muslims are supposed to be our enemies. They had to do something to make us fear these strangers in our midst."

And now, we are faced with how to respond, both to ISIS and to those refugees seeking lives of safety. How to confront the menace of ISIS itself I leave to others much more versed on the subject and capable of response. It must be a strong and unequivocal response; that much I know. But what, now, of those hundreds of thousands of refugees still fleeing, still desperately seeking sanctuary in some new home, including the United States?

The voices of fear in our own country, responding exactly as al-Baghdadi hoped, grow louder. They haunt; they distract; they needle their way into our consciousness. They are powerful voices, the voices of the kings of our society.

But we, here in this place, first and foremost, are Christian people. We are not Republicans or Democrats. We're not conservatives or liberals. We are not even Americans, not first. We are Christians. We are those who submit our very lives to the Gospel law of love. We are those who kneel before Christ the King. And our first question to ourselves must always be, "How would our King have us respond?"

"Who is my neighbor?" the lawyer asked Jesus. And Jesus told him a story of two people—a Jew and a Samaritan— from opposing religious traditions and cultures wary and suspicious of one another. Jesus chose as the emblematic picture of the Gospel of love one such person setting aside his own fears and needs in order to save the life of the other.[4]

Of the Syrian refugees being referred by the United Nations for settlement, more than half are children under the age of eighteen. It is worth mentioning, as we will be reminded during Advent, Jesus was himself once a child refugee seeking asylum from deadly violence across national boundaries. And the screening process for admitting refugees to the United States is rigorous, with the safety of United States citizens as top priority. At this point in time, it takes an average of eighteen to twenty-four months. Kathleen Newland, a senior fellow at the Migration Policy Institute says, "The refugee resettlement program is the least likely way for a terrorist to infiltrate the United States."[5]

The kings of this world—Abu Bakr al-Baghdadi, François Hollande, Barak Obama, Greg Abbott, take your pick—like David, they are but dust. They will pass; this crisis will pass; this era will pass. And someday there will be an exhibit somewhere that chronicles our response to these events. There will be photos and timelines. There may be vintage television sets looping interviews with the very voices crowding the news now. And, as with all later generations reflecting upon their priors, those who come after us will be, one way or the other, mystified by how we responded. It is my hope that they will be mystified—and inspired—by our willingness to love, to take absolutely seriously our role as subjects of Jesus our King.

Christ's kingdom does not decay. It is eternal, and we choose in every decision—personal and corporate—to whom we are subject. We are not called to be foolhardy. We are not called to be rash. But we are called, always and every time, to side with Christ the King and his love.

3

Skimming the Headlines

LUKE 10:38-42

JULY 17, 2016

*IN 2016, Columbia University reported that fifty-nine per-
cent of links shared on social media have never been read by
those who share them. As 2016 continued, this phenomenon
would only increase, with added charges and countercharges
of "fake news" and revelations that foreign actors sought to
influence the U.S. presidential election by capitalizing on the
American tendency to read headlines uncritically.*

"Scientists say giant asteroid could hit the earth next week,
causing mass devastation."[1] That headline screamed across
the online news feed on July 9th, 2016. The opening sentences of the story were these: "Scientists have discovered
a massive asteroid that is on course to hit the Earth next
week and are scrambling to find a way to divert the ob-
ject. The asteroid has been named 2016-FI and measures
approximately 1 km across. If it strikes a populated area,

it could wipe out entire cities and potentially devastate an entire continent."

As you might imagine, the story went viral. If we're faced with interstellar cataclysm, I suppose we should want the news to spread exponentially. I wonder if Home Depot saw a spike in sales of bomb shelter supplies.

And yet, here we are. The week of danger has passed with no asteroid, no Armageddon.

You see, the article turned out to be one-part news and another part social experiment. The news it shared had, it turns out, nothing to do with meteors. After those panicked opening sentences, the article revealed its actual content, a research study by Columbia University, which found that sixty percent of links shared on social media are never actually read by those who share them. Consider that. An almost supermajority of the online information in which so many of us traffic is passed along to others without being vetted, and often without even being read beyond the headline. As confirmation of the trend, the very article that announced it, with an inflammatory title and three supporting opening sentences about a cataclysmic asteroid, itself went viral.

The study's lead author says, "People are more willing to share an article than read it. This is typical of modern information consumption. People form an opinion based on a summary, or a summary of summaries, without making the effort to go deeper."

We ingest headlines without considering content. We absorb provocative statements, but we do not test their veracity. We allow our opinions and, indeed, our beliefs to be influenced by superlatives, but we too often fail to digest details, let alone analyze nuance.

The study and the article focused on online media, but the same phenomenon surely extends from the virtual into the everyday. We now, more than ever, live in a surface-skimming world, which is characterized by fast movement, speedy conclusions, and self-satisfying echo chambers in which we too often seek only the data—from media, from our leaders, from our circles of friends, indeed, from our church—that reinforces the things, theories, and conclusions we already *want* to be true.

This brings us to today's Gospel passage, about Martha and Mary. Most often this anecdote from Luke is interpreted as a case of competing virtues. Martha works for Jesus, while Mary communes with Jesus. Both are important, just as, for instance, volunteering at a support center for the homeless like The Beacon and attending worship are both important.

A quick search of books about Mary and Martha on Amazon.com suggests that the primary question we are supposed to ask is, "How can we best attend to both?" That's a fair question and one worth asking, but it is also a question that considers this passage out of context, and as such, it's not the question the passage itself implies to the reader. This passage is not primarily, I would suggest, a comparison of Martha's labor versus Mary's intimacy, so set that aside for the next few minutes. What, then, is it about?

In context, Jesus's visit to Martha and Mary immediately follows Jesus's Parable of the Good Samaritan. That parable flows directly into this story; there's not a single verse in between them. The Parable of the Good Samaritan, as the previous week's Lectionary reading reminded us, is Jesus's radical, grace-filled redefinition of our neighbors and our responsibilities to and for others as disciples of Jesus.

Its implications are profound for everything we do in the world, for our understanding of our responsibilities, and for our conception of the ways we both receive and extend love and grace to those around us. The Parable of the Good Samaritan can't be glossed over quickly, with the easy assumption that we understand its depths. It demands that we pause and take stock, that we read it again and again, even that we anguish over whether or not we want to believe and follow Jesus's words.

But in the very next verse—the very next verse—Martha pulls Jesus into her house, sits him down like an ornament, and moves on into the next room. She doesn't pause at all. She doesn't ask questions of Jesus. She doesn't wonder about the nuances of his teaching. She doesn't take stock of her own life and consider the transformation that may be required of her, of her values and her commitments in the world.

Martha only reads the headline, so to speak. To quote the Columbia University study with which I began, she makes no "effort to go deeper." Perhaps Martha believes she has Jesus figured out. Perhaps she assumes uncritically that whatever Jesus has to say will agree with, rather than challenge, the life she already lives. Martha becomes impatient with those who actually want to hear Jesus, to consider and understand him, to vet the whole article before living it and sharing it.

Not so, Mary. Mary is entranced and likely even perplexed by the words of Jesus. She can't go about her routine as usual, because the words of Jesus—not merely the easily misconstrued headlines but, more importantly, the heart of the Gospel message—have stopped her in her tracks. Luke doesn't tell us that Mary wants to give Jesus a warm hug, but that she wants to sit at his feet and listen.

Mary wants to understand the challenge that Jesus presents to her worldview. She wants to wrestle with what the Gospel means for the way she acts, interacts, speaks, believes, decides, cries, even sings—not just as she sits there in the comfort of her living room, but in every moment hereafter. Ultimately, Mary will share what she hears, and it will go viral like nothing our Internet has ever seen. But what she shares won't be a sound byte; or a willfully misinterpreted verse, wrenched from context; or a cozy platitude; or a half-baked theology that serves to undergird the way of life she already enjoys. Mary, who has taken the time to listen, who has made the effort to go deep and allow the words of Jesus to absorb into the marrow of her soul, will share the Gospel, the love of God-in-Christ that redefines everything.

St. Paul knows that Gospel. He shares it, too, and never more profoundly as in his Letter to the Colossians. If ever we wonder whether Jesus is merely a headline, to be slapped up and then quickly forgotten, listen to Paul:

> For in Christ all things in heaven and on earth were created, things visible and invisible, whether thrones or dominions or rulers or powers—all things have been created through him and for him. He himself is before all things, and in him all things hold together…Christ is the

beginning, the firstborn from the dead, so that
he might come to have first place in everything.
For in him all the fullness of God was pleased
to dwell, and through him God was pleased to
reconcile to himself all things, whether on earth
or in heaven.[2]

Jesus can't be skimmed. He can't be touted as a headline
in defense of some argument, or support of some theology,
or in reinforcement of a life already chosen. Jesus is the
whole thing, and we either take the whole of his Gospel of
crazy, radical, life-altering love in all of its implications, or
none of it. God knows, our world needs it.

Like Mary, we must be entranced, perplexed, and chal-
lenged to sit at Jesus's feet and listen, so that we can be
changed. As transformed people, we are then to go into
the world and share the words that are to "have first place
in everything," through which Jesus "reconciles to himself
all things," and by which we encounter grace and find our
lives in God.

4

9/11, Fifteen Years Later

LUKE 15:1-10

SEPTEMBER 11, 2016

ON SEPTEMBER 11, 2001, nearly three thousand people were killed and six thousand injured in coordinated terrorist attacks on the World Trade Center in New York, the Pentagon in Washington, D.C., and on United Airlines Flight 93, which crashed outside of Shanksville, Pennsylvania. The 9/11 attacks killed more Americans than Pearl Harbor. 9/11 defined a generation and continues to influence U.S. foreign and domestic policy today. On the fifteenth anniversary of 9/11, Christ Church Cathedral inaugurated a new Celtic Sunday evening Eucharist, The Well.

As we gather for the inaugural celebration of our Celtic service, The Well, this evening is auspicious, and it holds some tension. On the one hand, we come together for the first time in this style of worship, which is both ancient in our tradition and new to Christ Church Cathedral. We sing, pause, and pray in ways intending to remind us of God's deep peace that runs—like water from a sacred well—beneath all of the things on the surface of our lives that seek to disrupt our equanimity. On the other hand, we observe today the fifteenth anniversary of that singular event of our lifetimes, which spoke so powerfully that we had—and still have—difficulty finding words to counteract the horror: September 11, 2001.

In 2005, Richard Lischer wrote a book entitled *The End of Words*. His thesis is that our world has become so violent, so unpredictable, so chaotic, so insane that words have lost their inherent meaning. Words are now but tools in the hands of those who wish to manipulate other people. As a lover and crafter of words, it pains me to agree with this notion. But too often today, publicly and privately, words are combined to fool, frighten, or whip into frenzy. And, each time this happens, we feel, like the hundredth sheep in Jesus's parable, a bit more lost.

Religious words are among the most manipulated, and perhaps never more so than on and immediately after 9/11. Some during those days invoked the Prince of Peace to sound drums of war. On the opposite extreme, others utilized the Gospel to suggest that we'd brought terror on ourselves, as if we deserved that awful day. Both extremes made the rest of us feel as if we were cast ever further from the sheep herd, more and more lost in some strange wilderness.

But the most abused religious words spoken on and around 9/11 were those of the hijackers themselves. On United Airlines Flight 93, the terrorists were recorded saying—as they killed the pilots and ultimately crashed the plane in a Pennsylvania field—"In the name of God, the most merciful, the most compassionate…O, God, the most gracious."[1]

Former Archbishop of Canterbury Rowan Williams says, "[These] religious words are, in the cold light of day, the words [of] murderers [used] in order to make a martyr's drama out of a crime."[2]

In a world where the most holy and sacred words are used so cynically, so dishonestly, how can we ever put our faith in words at all?

But, lest we forget, there were other words that day. From airplanes and from the Twin Towers, dozens of trapped people telephoned family members, friends, and sometimes mere strangers on the other end of the line. Invariably, the words spoken on such calls are words of love.[3]

It isn't surprising that some of these calls express panic. What *is* surprising is the large percentage of them that evidence a remarkable calm, even as steel collapses in wrecked buildings or hijackers scream in the background. The recipients of the calls have fear in their voices. But the callers are more often steely and intent:

A newlywed says to her father, "Dad, you have to find Sean and tell him that I love him."

A young professional says to his mother, "I love you no matter what happens."

The voicemail message a woman leaves for her husband records, "There's a lot of smoke, and I just wanted you to know that I love you always."

These words overpower those other words of war and blame and terror. Archbishop Williams says of those trapped in the Twin Towers and on the planes,

> Someone who is about to die in terrible anguish makes room in [his] mind for someone else; for the grief and terror of someone [he] loves. [He] does what [he] can to take some atom of that pain away from the other by the inarticulate message on the mobile [phone]…These non-religious words are testimony to what religious language is supposed to be about—the triumph of pointless, gratuitous love, the affirming of faithfulness even when there is nothing to be done or salvaged.[4]

Perhaps never have we felt more like lost sheep than on September 11, 2001, when the planes crashed and the towers crumbled. But we know that love never stops seeking the lost sheep. We know that love will not give up. We discover again in those telephone messages that, even lost in the wilderness, even on the smoky 89th floor, even nose-down on a doomed airplane, love abides.

And what is love but God, and specifically the Incarnate Jesus over whom death has no power? With love—with the Christ of God, with *that* Word—we can emerge from any wilderness, found and embraced by the Well of Life.

In my memory, the word "triumph" was used too often around 9/11. But what would it mean if we affirmed, with Archbishop Williams, that *love* triumphed that day? Pointless, gratuitous love: love that does not panic, love that does not run away, love that seeks the lost, love that is faithful in the face of any threat. As we prayerfully reflect on this fifteen-years-past, and as we look forward into the wildernesses ahead, we'll know which words are those of the God of love. And when we hear them, we'll remember that we are never lost.

5

The Election, God, and Our Bliss

LUKE 20:27-38

NOVEMBER 6, 2016

AFTER THE 2016 PRESIDENTIAL CAMPAIGN, the Pew Research Center polled the American public on its assessment of the ways the candidates, pollsters, and the press had conducted themselves.[1] *Respondents gave each category the lowest grades since Pew began collecting such data thirty years ago. Seemingly daily during the election cycle, standards of common human decency diminished. On the one hand, candidates were willing to say anything to win. On the other hand, revelations of some candidates' behavior, which in prior election cycles would have disqualified one from office in the minds of voters, were instead celebrated by supporters. The campaign led many to despair that something had been irretrievably lost in the American consciousness.*

When my wife, Jill, our kids, and I lived in Roanoke, Virginia, we were frequent visitors to the Busch Gardens amusement park in Williamsburg. Griffin loved the roller coasters; Eliza loved the water rides; and Jill and I enjoyed the European themes. We could visit England, Italy, and France without ever boarding an airplane.

The park was always crowded, and the year we visited during spring break, it was crushingly so. Eliza was five years old. She was very small, and as we walked through the park, her hand in mine was feather light. There is one spot in Busch Gardens that forms a bottleneck, funneling a huge volume of people through a relatively narrow archway as you approach the miniature cars, an area both our kids loved.

That spring break, as Eliza and I passed through the arch, suddenly the feel of her tiny hand in mine disappeared. I looked down, and she was not there. In the crush of people and movement, she was gone.

Time stopped. The workings of my imagination went into overdrive, considering a dozen panicked possibilities in a split second: She has been taken. She has been trampled. She has been erased from the earth. My complacent bliss turned, in an instant, into fear, confusion, and an unfamiliar sense that I hadn't a clue what to do next.

Eliza's smiling face emerged from the crowd one second later, and I picked her up—thank God—with a bear hug of relief. If you are a parent, or if you have ever loved anyone in your life, you know how I felt in that moment when Eliza's tiny hand was drawn from my grasp.

Since that day years ago, I don't recall experiencing anything akin to this emotion until—and I do not offer this as a joke—the lead up to Tuesday's presidential election. For a time, I suspected I was being histrionic or overwrought, until other people began coming out of the woodwork to share their similar emotional responses with me.

People on the right and on the left, both Trumpeters and the "I'm with Hillary" army—and the broad swath in between—feel as if something precious, something held perhaps too lightly for too long, may be about to slip from our grasp. We wonder if we've been too complacent in our bliss. We are anxious and confused, and, depending on the outcome of Tuesday's election, we don't have a clue as to what we're supposed to do next.

I've been thinking on the word "bliss" lately. When Sister Joan Chittister was at Christ Church Cathedral for a Faith and Reason Seminar in mid-October, she reminded us that the Beatitudes, which we read on this All Saints Sunday, rightly refer to our bliss. We usually read "Blessed are they…" with the idea, either conscious or subconscious, that the "blessing" refers to some reward in the next life. "Bless-ed" becomes "blest," and the Beatitudes are then understood as the hope of heaven. "Blest are the poor, for theirs is the kingdom of God" is interpreted like the Parable of Lazarus and the Rich Man, as if to say, "In the great hereafter the poor will receive heavenly riches, so in the end it's all going to be OK for them."

I certainly believe and hope it will be, but that interpretation lends us an excuse to say of that long list of people, both good and bad, included in the Beatitudes, "We need not worry about them. God will take care of it all eventually."

Sister Joan pointed out to us that this understanding is a gross misreading of the Beatitudes' intent. "Bless-ed," an etymological study quickly reveals, is best interpreted "blissful." And that casts a different light entirely on the

Beatitudes. The Beatitudes are all about, regardless of the circumstances we experience, *where we find our bliss.*

Matthew's Beatitudes focus on our spirits, while Luke's focus on our bodies, but this truth holds in either case: Our anxieties, our hungers, our tears, our struggles in this life are also those very depths in which we most often discover, to our utter and complete surprise, that we tap into the well-spring of God. It is in those experiences that, even through our pain, we encounter bliss, that "peace which passes all understanding," as St. Paul calls it.[2]

It is in the belly of the whale, at the bottom of the sea, we recall, that Jonah sings his salvation song.[3] When all else is stripped from us, God is there, waiting in love. There we find our bliss.

Even so, it would be a mistake to think that this bliss, this peace, this resting in the heart of God intends to lull us into complacency. Immediately after sharing the Beatitudes, Jesus tells us what the encounter with God's deep grace compels us to do: Do good to those who hate you; bless those who curse you; pray for those who abuse you. Give to those in need, and do so with gratitude for the blessings you bear. Be kind, and be merciful. Our own deep need, which leads to our own deep bliss, compels us to identify in solidarity with the grave concerns and needs of others.

This is not merely a posture we are to slip into on Sunday mornings. It is a way of being in the world. It changes how we see ourselves and how we see others. The Christian spiritual writer Henri Nouwen says that this shift in our understanding is "the movement in which we become less and less fearful and defensive and more and more open to other people and their worlds."[4]

As we approach election day, we fear that our bliss is slipping away. But Jesus tells us insistently that we have found our bliss in the wrong places. Our bliss is not found in our material things, or our societal privileges, or our nation's military might, or the presumed superiority of our political opinions. Our bliss, the deep peace that endures through all dangers, all uncertainties, all election cycles, rightly finds its source in our connection to the God of love, and that eternal bliss leads us to deep compassion and concern for all of God's people in this world.

We should start there, before we vote, before we obsess over the election results that pour in on Tuesday evening, and surely before we react to whatever new world we find ourselves in on Wednesday morning. God's bliss is not feather light. It bears the weight of glory, and it cannot slip from our grasp, come what may.

6

The Mystic Chords:
Post-Election Thoughts

ISAIAH 65:17-25, LUKE 21:5-19

NOVEMBER 13, 2016

ON NOVEMBER 8, 2016, Donald J. Trump defeated Hillary Clinton to become the forty-fifth President of the United States. Trump won the Electoral College, 304-227. Clinton won the popular vote 48.2%-46.1%. The immediate reaction of some to the election results was an extension of behavior during the campaign, which one commentator called, "the most bitter in recent American history."[1]

As a kid, every afternoon I watched reruns of the 1960s sitcom "Get Smart" on Super Station WTBS. At the most crucial moments of discernment and decision, Max, Agent 99, and the Chief would sit across a table and activate "the cone of silence." The futuristic, plexiglass cone would descend from the ceiling to envelop all the conversation partners in a quiet space, impenetrable by outside ears.

But the cone never worked correctly. It was an echo chamber. Rather than facilitating listening, the cone of silence prevented anyone inside from hearing anyone else. Max, Agent 99, and the Chief could make out only a word here or a phrase there, and through their partial hearing they often came to the wrong conclusions. They ended up frustrated and confused, unable to determine how to move forward. At the very moment in which listening to one another was most important, the characters created conditions in which listening was impossible.

On the Wednesday morning after Election Day, roughly half of the voters in our nation were relieved at the outcome of the presidential race, while the other half were shocked and saddened. Both sides immediately called down the proverbial cone of silence, in which the echo chamber completely cut them off from hearing any divergent voices. Consequently, we have thus far heard only the sounds of our own disappointment or joy, fear or relief. Indeed, more than a few people—again, representing both sides of the divide—have actually and honestly said to me that they aren't interested in hearing from someone who cast a vote different from their own. In our digital day and age that avoidance is easy. Our cones of silence are so impermeable that even the Facebook algorithm, we now know, sends us only those news items that track with our own already-expressed opinions.

This across-the-board response is the fevered extension of what was surely the most toxic election cycle in my lifetime, and perhaps in our nation's history. Epithets and reckless speech, first lobbed from the top, bounced down until common citizens began to believe the worst motives of one another. Sound bytes prevailed; real conversation among people ceased; and, even among folks who'd known each other for years, suspicion began to take root. At the Dean's Hour forum here at the Cathedral just last week, Ambassador Linnet Deily shared poignantly, "I've never seen an election that has divided friends and family such as this has."

Of course, such a failure to listen becomes a self-fulfilling prophecy. It is human nature that when one feels unheard, one begins to speak more loudly, more vociferously, with less care, and with greater abandon. Since Election Day, some elements among both the relieved and the fearful have responded in ways that should concern us deeply.

On one side of the divide, news outlets report numerous instances of threat and actual physical assault across the country against Muslims, Latinos, and African-Americans. Perhaps most distressingly, several of these events have occurred in high schools and middle schools, which reveal the extent to which our children hear the bits and pieces of our rhetoric and respond in their contexts. It is as if we have forgotten that we form our children in particular ways by careless words. They are mirrors for us, and we should see ourselves in their actions.[2] People of color and religious minorities are afraid, and their fear is real. They wonder if the America they thought they knew—and in many cases the American dream that drew them here—is an illusion.

On the other side, CBS News reports that a man in Chicago was pulled from his car and assaulted after a traffic altercation, while his attackers vocally cited the man's support for Donald Trump as their motivation.[3] National

Public Radio reports that the protests of the past few days in some American cities have becomes riots, with rioters attacking both police and the very livelihoods of small business owners, engaging in, according to police, "criminal and dangerous behavior."[4]

In preparation for the fall Dean's Hour series, I have spent the past several months studying the faith, lives, and leadership of four of the greatest presidents who ever served our country. As I have struggled through this election cycle, their words have sustained me in ways I did not expect. During this election week, as I have watched our nation and felt the echo chamber descend, the words of Abraham Lincoln's First Inaugural Address have come back to me again and again. On the cusp of conflict far deeper than our own, the President reminded his fellow citizens:

> We are not enemies, but friends. We must not be enemies. Though passion may have strained, it must not break our bonds of affection. The mystic chords of memory, stretching from every battle-field, and patriot grave, to every living heart and hearth-stone, all over this broad land, will yet swell the chorus of the Union, when again touched, as surely they will be, by the better angels of our nature.[5]

This begins here, at Christ Church Cathedral and places like it. Here, we must model the better angels of our nature. For us, of course, Lincoln's mystic chords of memory extend all the way back to the days of Jesus and Isaiah. They are our inspirations and models; they, and not today's political candidates or elected officials, are the ones who rightly form our beliefs, our convictions, and our actions. It is either serendipity or grace that in today's lectionary readings both the Prophet and the Savior remind us of what God will do in the midst of turbulent times. Isaiah shares with us God's promise to "create a new heaven and a new earth," one in which distress and weeping are heard no more. But, friends, until the Lord returns, the vanguard of that new heaven and new earth is no one but us.

"The mystic chords of memory...will yet swell the chorus of the Union, when again touched, as surely they will be, by the better angels of our nature."

This is daunting, and never more so than in conflicted times. But Jesus promises that he will grant us words and wisdom that no one can withstand or contradict. As the election approached, I sought to convey the character and content of those words and that wisdom in my sermons. I conveyed St. Paul's last will and testament, when Paul says, in the end, all that matters is that we hold fast to the faith and love of Jesus, and share it in all our words and actions.[6]

I also spoke about the bliss of communion with God that is felt most deeply when we recognize, in our most vulnerable moments, how we are connected with all who suffer and are vulnerable. Not when you and I are strong and triumphant, Jesus says, but when we are weak, or afraid, or on the very precipice of life is the time to take note of that experience, so that we always remember, in both times of strength and weakness, to do good to those with whom we disagree; to stand up for those in need; to be kind, and be merciful.[7]

As long as Christ Church Cathedral endures, I pray we will do these things, not because of politics on the right or the left, but because the prophets and the Savior compel us. What does it mean to be Christians, after all, other than to follow the Way of Jesus? I pray we will deny the echo chamber and listen to those who differ from us. That will not always lead to agreement—nor should it—but it will move us toward understanding and away from imputing false motives to one another. And I pray we will, without doubt or hesitation, stand with and for all of God's children who are vulnerable and fearful in this world, whatever their color, creed, religion, lifestyle, or political belief.

As I considered this sermon, I read a remarkable blog post[8] by Riaz Patel, a Muslim, Pakistani-American, gay man who supported Hillary Clinton. In the weeks leading up to this election, Mr. Patel wanted to shed his echo chamber, to hear and understand those who supported Donald Trump. So Mr. Patel traveled to Ketchikan, Alaska to visit with third-generation fishermen who were themselves fearful of economic displacement from proposed environmental regulations that would upend their ability to make a living from the sea. In a diner called The Landing, Mr. Patel and his husband broke bread with locals Nicole, Jim, and Paula. Together, they were a motley crew who could not have been more different, but they all spoke openly. They all shared their fears and concerns. In their conversation, the mystic chords held, and the better angels of their nature prevailed. I daresay that neither Mr. Patel nor his conversation partners changed their vote, but I have no doubt that their connection altered the way they saw one another and, God willing, their commitment to one another in time of trial and need.

We do well to embrace the words of Jesus and the words of those two prophets, Isaiah and Abraham Lincoln. Today, tomorrow, next year, and until the Lord returns, we are called by God to embody the better angels of our nature. We are called to shed our echo chambers and listen to those who differ from us, to see the best in them and hope the best for them. We are called to stand unequivocally with those who are vulnerable. We are called to receive grace and reflect grace. In these ways, and no others, will the mystic chords and bonds of affection that bind us as a nation be preserved. In these ways, and no others, will we be the vanguard of God's new heaven and new earth.

7 O'Clock News

MATTHEW 1:18-25

DECEMBER 8, 2016

AS 2016 CAME TO AN END, many were exhausted by the acrimony, anxiety, and fear that had characterized the year. Simon and Garkfunkel's "7 O'Clock News" provided context that the turmoil of our time is not unprecedented—and not even all that rare—as well as the reminder of God's constantly renewed promise to be in the midst of us.

Exactly fifty years ago in 1966, Paul Simon and Art Garfunkel released their third studio album, *Parsley, Sage, Rosemary and Thyme*. The record was a hit and consists of an eclectic playlist that includes the wistful "Homeward Bound," the conflicted "Dangling Conversation," and the light-hearted "Feelin' Groovy." The final track on the album surprised many first-time listeners, because it differs from all the others in both substance and style. It begins as a traditional Christmas carol:

Silent night, holy night;
all is calm, all is bright.
Round yon virgin, mother and child;
holy infant so tender and mild…

As soon as it begins, however, the carol is interrupted by background static overlaid on the track, almost as if a second radio station is interfering with the song. As the song goes on, the background voice becomes louder and more distinct. It says something about President Lyndon Johnson and the civil rights bill. Slowly the listener realizes that the voice is a newscaster, whose first clearly discernable statement is "In Los Angeles today, comedian Lenny Bruce died of what was believed to be a narcotics overdose. Bruce was forty-two years old."

At that point, as if in rebellion against the bad news, the duet's voices crescendo:

Sleep in heavenly peace; sleep in heavenly peace.

But the newscaster drones on, ever louder:

Dr. Martin Luther King says he does not intend to cancel plans for an open housing march Sunday into the Chicago suburb of Cicero… The police in Cicero said they would ask that the National Guard be called out if it is held… In Chicago, Richard Speck, accused murderer of nine student nurses, was brought before a grand jury today for indictment. The nurses were found stabbed and strangled in their Chicago apartment.

And so it goes. The news gets worse, if you can believe it. The newscaster reports stories about Vietnam and anti-war protests. He mentions the conspiratorial theories of Congress's Un-American Activities Committee. The tumult of the news attempts to take center stage, but all the while Simon and Garfunkel will not allow the light in their harmony to be snuffed. They claim the sound waves:

Silent night, holy night;
all is calm, all is bright.

Round yon virgin, mother and child;
holy infant, so tender and mild.
Sleep in heavenly peace;
sleep in heavenly peace.

The newscaster ends by saying, "That's the 7 o'clock edition of the news. Goodnight," as Simon and Garfunkel's last refrain echoes in the air.

The final track on *Parsley, Sage, Rosemary and Thyme*, titled "7 O'Clock News" is masterful. It expertly captures the tension of Advent, which existed fifty years ago in 1966, existed two thousand years ago in Palestine, and still exists today. In Matthew today, we read the precious story that the Holy Spirit of God conceives with Mary, and an angel of the Lord announces to Joseph that this child will be Emmanuel, God-with-us. With the angel's annunciation comes the nascent hope that God's promises will be fulfilled. We wait all year for this reading. We wait all year to kneel and sing "Silent Night," on Christmas Eve and to rest in the warm and hopeful glow of the Christ Child's birth.

But we also live in the world. And our newscasters, *this* Advent, seek to drown out the blessed melody with reports of ongoing violence in Syria, as well as dozens of Coptic Christians—the world's oldest enduring Christian sect— being blown up within their ancient cathedral by terrorists in Egypt. The newscasters tell us of Russians hacking our political system. They report on the ominous rise of old prejudices and racially motivated hate groups that we had hoped were long gone. And, increasingly, they reveal that some of our news isn't even news, but rather consists of stories fabricated whole cloth to discredit and sow fear and manipulate people.

Yes, we live in a fearful and uncertain world at a fearful and uncertain time. The question for us—the pivotal Advent question—is which do we believe has the final say: the Nativity or the newscast? Which do we believe prevails in the end?

The angel's first words to Joseph are "Do not be afraid." The angel says the same to Mary in Luke's version of the story.[1] It is also the repeated refrain of Jesus to the disciples throughout the Gospels whenever the world seems about to overwhelm them.[2] *Do not be afraid.*

But Jesus and the angel don't offer this encouragement to pretend that everything in these days will work out OK. They do not mean that every cancer will be healed, every job preserved, that every politician will earn our trust, every social fracture will mend, or all religious violence will end. Mary's heart, after all, is broken along with Jesus's

70

body on the cross. The angel's promise at the annunciation does not prevent her real and deep pain at the crucifixion.

Our encouragement to fear not is, rather, the promise that, since that first Advent, since the Incarnation of God on Christmas, we do not walk through this world alone. Our courage comes not from the illusion of well-being provided by rose-colored glasses, but from the sure knowledge that even if we walk through fire in this world, God is with us. Emmanuel. No matter the 7 o'clock newscast, no matter the static it overlays on our days, no matter how loud its bad news, the sacred melody always also plays. It will not be drowned out. God is with us.

And there is more, even, than that. Advent is not only about looking backward to the Nativity. It is also about looking forward to Christ's return, to that day on the far side of the newscast, beyond the worst the world can throw at God's children, when God will finally say, "Enough!" and the one who begins as the babe in the manger will reign in love over all things.

After the newscast forever ends, the carol's final refrain will go on, not as an echo, but as the world's only truth. That is Advent hope. That is what we are to anticipate with expectancy. Believe it, friends, and do not be afraid.

8

All Israel Will Be Saved

ROMANS 11:1-2, 29-32

AUGUST 20, 2017

ON AUGUST 12, 2017, white nationalists converged on Charlottesville, Virginia, under the pretext of protesting the planned removal of a Robert E. Lee statue. The rally served, in fact, as a public display of racism and bigotry in many forms. Two months before, The Atlantic Monthly *ran a lengthy piece on white nationalist Richard Spencer, whose bigotries proudly include anti-Semitism.*

2017 also marked the five hundredth anniversary of the Lutheran Reformation. In observance of that anniversary, a group of Cathedral parishioners traveled to Wittenberg, Germany, on pilgrimage, where the history lesson included a cautionary reminder of the danger of resurgent bigotry in our own day.

In June 2017, forty-two Cathedral parishioners and I traveled to Wittenberg, Germany, to pray, learn, and pay homage to the five-hundredth anniversary of the Protestant Reformation. We walked through that picturesque village to the City Church, where Martin Luther pastored and preached for decades in the sixteenth century. In the sacristy of the church we held a prayer service and raised our voices to God in praise. It was a remarkable experience that crossed time, space, and language and reminded us of the Communion of Saints, the great cloud of witnesses to God's love, grace, and mercy of which we are a part.

After the service, we left the church through a side door and entered the courtyard. As we looked up at the church façade, we saw there, in a place of prominence and even honor, the most grotesque sculpture I've ever seen. It is not a traditional gargoyle. It is not even some hellish scene of the damned such as one finds in the Duomo in Florence. No, what we saw on Martin Luther's church, in the very crucible of the Reformation, was a *Judensau*.

The word means in English what it sounds like in German: Jewish pig. Rather than attempting to describe the sculpture, I will share Martin Luther's own description, which he wrote in 1543:

> Here on our church in Wittenberg, a sow is sculpted in stone. Piglets and Jews lie suckling under her. Behind the sow a rabbi is bent over the sow, lifting up her right leg, holding her tail high and looking intensely under her tail and into her...which is certainly where [the Jews] get their [understanding of God].[1]

The Judensau was installed on the City Church in 1305, high and prominent so that it could not be missed. Two hundred years later, the Father of the Reformation praised it and joked about its humiliating depiction of Jews.

Does that shock you? It did us. That evening at our hotel, our group's memory of worship in City Church, so sublime just a few hours before, had faded. The day's experience that stayed with us, that made us fidgety and uncomfortable, that we felt compelled to verbalize (and yet for which we had difficulty finding words), was of that sculpture, through which centuries of Christians who claimed God's love, grace, and mercy also proclaimed that Jews were animals, that their understanding of God was nothing more than what would come from the tail end of swine, and that they were beyond the bounds of salvation.

The debate within Christianity about the status and stature of Jews goes back more than a millennium before the Judensau was installed on Wittenberg's City Church, all the way to the decades just after the Resurrection. In fact, that debate is a primary reason that St. Paul wrote his Letter to the Romans. Under the reign of Roman Emperor Claudius in the first century, Jews were expelled from Rome. During their absence, the young Christian Church in Rome gained ground; after the Emperor died and the Jews returned, Christians began arguing among themselves about the Jews.

Now that Jesus had died and been resurrected, they asked, were the Jews still God's chosen people? Weren't Jews cut off from God, now and forever?

Paul is never one to avoid the hardest questions, and he tackles this issue head-on. First, Paul reminds his fellow

Christians that they themselves do not *deserve* God's grace. They haven't earned it. They haven't achieved it. In fact, it's not even their faith that leads to their salvation. Rather, it's the faith Jesus demonstrated in his allegiance to God and his willingness to undergo the Passion that leads to anyone's salvation. Note that: Paul says it is not our faith that saves us. It is Jesus's faith that saves us, and saves anyone.[2]

Paul then constructs the metaphor of a foot race toward salvation.[3] He says that though the Jews took off from the starting blocks, they stumbled along the way. But the gentiles, he adds, never took off at all. When the whistle sounded, they sat idly by, picking daisies. Paul is scathing in his ridicule. The mental image is of all the runners— Christians, Jews, everybody—bumbling around like the Keystone Cops. Out of such a human mess, which describes our world as much as Paul's, no one could achieve communion with God, either in this world or the next. Only through *God's* action, not our own, can *anyone* find God.

And then Paul comes to his conclusion about the Jews. Yes, Paul believes in the centrality of Jesus. Yes, Paul's own faith in Jesus has changed his entire life. And yet, Paul says in today's reading from Romans 11, including a few verses that the Lectionary omits, "I ask you, then, has God rejected his people? By no means! ...So that you may not claim to be wiser than you are, brothers, and sisters, I want you to understand a mystery...all Israel will be saved! ... for the gifts and the calling of God are irrevocable. "[4]

With power, Paul's declaration echoes through time. It shakes the foundation of the City Church in Wittenberg. It should make the soul of Martin Luther shudder, he who so loved the Letter to the Romans but failed to receive all its truth.

Paul is speaking specifically of the Jews, but the truth is broader than that: Who God redeems, and how God accomplishes that redemption, is up to God, not us. And while we should surely rejoice in our communion with God and effusively share that joy with others, it is ridiculous—literally worthy of Paul's ridicule—for us to act as if we get to decide, or even that we know, to whom God extends love, grace, and mercy.

Why does this matter now? Here is why: Just a few days after we visited Wittenberg, our group made pilgrimage to the Nazi concentration camp at Dachau. In the 1500s, Martin Luther, Father of the Reformation, gave his casual assent to, and then participated in, the denigration of a minority group—both ethnic and religious—that was vulnerable and lacked power in society. And there is a direct historic line between the anti-Judaism of Martin Luther's day and the deadly anti-Semitism of Hitler's Germany. The former morphed into the latter. And Germany is not a unique example. Again and again in Christian history, among those with power and privilege in society, the pretension of superiority and the religious arrogance of one generation, when unchecked, morphs into the scapegoating and persecution of a later generation.

As I stated at the outset, we belong, across time and space, to the Communion of Saints. But we also belong to a communion of sinners. For good or ill, we are connected to the Christians of Luther's Wittenberg. And, we are connected to the Christians in our own country's past, who sometimes misunderstood and abused the Gospel to afflict and dispirit others. We inherit the legacy of both communions, saints and sinners, good and bad. We surely celebrate the virtues of the past; but if we deny or ignore its sins—or fail to take care with the words we use, the claims we make, and the stands we take or reject—we risk allowing these sins of the past to gestate and be reborn in the future in even more destructive forms.

Today, we find ourselves in another time in which suspicion, vitriol, and the scapegoating of people of different religions, ethnicities, races, and orientations are all on the rise. How are we to respond? With silence? With casual acquiescence? With behind-closed-doors participation in support of bigotry and hate?

I pray we will respond as people who know that we are redeemed by the grace of God and not by anything we deserve or do. I pray we'll respond as people who believe St. Paul's message that God's abundant grace extends to people we might not expect and in ways that are a mystery to us. I pray we'll respond with love, extending our arms wide to embrace, and honor, and protect when necessary, all of God's children.

In other words, I pray we'll respond as followers of Jesus.

9

"I Will Send You":
In the Wake of Hurricane Harvey

EXODUS 3:1-15

SEPTEMBER 3, 2017

HURRICANE HARVEY MADE LANDFALL on August 25, 2017 as a Category 4 storm. Harvey dumped twenty-seven trillion gallons of rain on Texas and did more than $125 billion in damage, ranking it the second costliest storm in United States history after Hurricane Katrina. Thirteen million people were adversely affected by Harvey. One hundred thirty-five thousand homes were damaged or destroyed, as were one million automobiles. Harvey's ultimate death toll was eighty-eight people.[1]

The disaster has happened. It is a concrete fact that cannot be altered or undone. A bright day turned to shadow; and, by the time the clouds lifted, everything had changed. In the wake of tragedy, the question is "What happens next?"

This describes the experience of Hurricane Harvey and its wake. It also describes, exactly, where Moses finds himself in Exodus 3. The Book of Genesis ended on a sunny and bright note. Jacob and his sons had left their land of famine and traveled to Egypt, where they not only discovered grain in plenty, but also Joseph, Jacob's lost son, who had risen in rank from slave to become the governor of all Egypt. But Joseph died, and over time the relationship of the Egyptians to the Hebrews soured. Jacob's descendants became an underclass. Then, they were enslaved. And, finally, when Pharaoh felt threatened by their numbers, their baby boys were killed. Sunlight turned to shadow.

Moses survived because his mother's love was as shrewd as it was powerful, and Moses was raised as an Egyptian. As he grew, Moses despaired at the conditions all around him, and he eventually fled, until, Exodus tells us today, he was "beyond the wilderness." This is biblical speak for telling us Moses was out of options, and so frayed he couldn't think straight, and all alone, and on the very edge of panic. Moses wondered in his exhaustion, "What happens next?"

Very like us. Skies were sunny, and Houston was a shining emblem of that which is good in our country. And then the world ended. Beginning on August 25, 2017, and continuing for days, Houston experienced more than fifty-one inches of rain. That's more than twenty-four trillion gallons, breaking every US record. Harvey also retained tropical storm force longer than any storm in Texas history. If Harvey's rain had been snow, the snow would have reached forty-two feet. That's level height, not snow drifts.[2] More than three hundred thousand people have already applied for FEMA relief. Forty-two thousand people are presently housed in shelters. Forty people have died to date. Rockport was devastated. Beaumont drowned. One runs out of superlative adjectives to describe things, and then one simply runs out of the energy to speak at all. By last Monday night, many Texans—including a fair number of our own parishioners and the roughly three hundred downtown homeless men and women who rely on The Beacon's homeless services for water and food—were out of options. They were so frayed they couldn't think straight, they were all alone, and they were on the very edge of panic. We all wondered, "What happens next?"

For Moses, what happens next is most unexpected. In the wake of disaster, beyond the wilderness, when everything is stripped bare, Moses meets God. God appears in a bush that burns but is not consumed, and we mustn't let the power of that metaphor escape us: The powers of nature are great and fierce, but they cannot touch the power of God. God says to Moses the very words Moses longs to hear. God says, "I have seen the misery of my people. I have heard them crying out. I know their suffering. And I have come to deliver them." Sweeter words were never spoken. Sweeter words were never heard.

But lest Moses exhale, relieved that God will deliver him and his kinsman and wondering vaguely how God will accomplish this, in God's very next utterance God says to Moses, "I will send you."

Very like us. By Tuesday morning, flotillas of boats replaced this city's deluged cars. The George R. Brown opened its doors. The Coast Guard sent helicopters. And thousands upon thousands of Houstonians responded to the call of God. "What happens next?" we ask. And God responds, "I will send you."

I want to tell you some stories. Three mornings after the storm began, I worked the breakfast shift at the evacuee shelter at the George R. Brown Convention Center. The Red Cross is skeptical of clergy volunteers, fearing that pastors will attempt to proselytize evacuees (even though I explained to them that Episcopalians don't really do that). As I visited with people, hearing their experiences, a man in street clothes named Bob Merrill approached me to tell me that he is an Episcopal priest. I said to Bob, "You were smart not to wear your collar; the Red Cross won't question you." To which Bob responded, "Oh, I don't have my collar. I was flooded out. I'm mainly here as an evacuee, but I'm also trying to help." He'd lost everything, and his first instinct was to his calling: *I will send you.*

Chris and Alison Bell's home was flooded this week for the third time in as many years, but, as for everyone, this time was far worse. The Bells' flood drill had almost become routine. Chris and Alison and their sons, Atlee, and Connally, moved to the second story as the water crept in. But this time the water didn't stop rising. Eventually, a boat plucked Chris and Alison, their sons, and their dogs from the house; but next the Bells endured a rain-soaked ride in the back of a county dump truck before being left on the side of the road shivering alone in darkness.

Finally, the headlamps of a jeep emerged, and a young man named Brandon, a stranger, picked up the Bells and navigated a slow path to safety. The Bells' saga was long, meandering, and frightening, but when I talked to Chris two days later, this is what stayed with him: "Every time I [think of] Brandon, our rescuer, I start tearing up. It's overwhelming when one realizes there really are saints among us. He came from nowhere at a time when four people and three dogs were incredibly cold and helpless. Perhaps not from nowhere." God says, *I will send you.*

One more: Throughout the storm, I worried about the Cathedral campus. I take the stewardship of this historic and sacred space very seriously, and I feared both floodwaters and bad actors. On Sunday, our head sexton, Ardell Ray, had made it to the Cathedral before the water rose too high. But, on Monday, Ardell had to go back home to check on his own house, and he barely made it; his car nearly stalled in water on the way. So, on Monday afternoon I put on my rain boots and decided to try and drive downtown to check on the Cathedral myself.

Before I could do so, Ardell called. That was odd: Ardell takes my calls, but he rarely calls me. He was on his bicycle, pedaling through the city in the storm at a snail's pace, making his way back downtown to protect this holy place. "Dean," Ardell said, "You don't have to worry about a thing. I'm going to take good care of it." And God says, *I will send you.*

When God tells Moses that Moses is to be the instrument of deliverance, Moses's momentary relief turns to anxiety and terror. Moses is inadequate to the task, he tells God. He has not the voice, the skill, or the will to do what God says must be done. And God does not disagree. But rather than removing the responsibility from Moses, God gives Moses Aaron, recognizing that none of us can navigate the storms, and none of us can deliver one another, without all of us.

God hears our cry. God takes note of our suffering. And though the power of Hurricane Harvey was mighty, it was no match for God. *I will send you*, God says to us. So, what happens next?

Here's what happens: Fellow parishioner Seth Hinkley has accepted the call to serve as our Cathedral Hurricane Relief Coordinator and parishioner Gary Krause has agreed to assist Seth. Beginning tomorrow, Seth and Gary will coordinate all of our parish relief efforts.

We will have ample resources with which to do this work. In the past five days, the Cathedral has received more than twenty thousand dollars in hurricane relief contributions, and more funds are streaming in.[3] Every dollar will be used to help those in need. We will help with housing; we will help with transportation; we will help with groceries; we will help in whatever ways help is needed.

We will open the Ballard Youth Center as temporary housing for relief and restoration work crews from across the country in the coming weeks and months.

These things we will do, but we have not waited until now to respond to God's call. Since the middle of last week, Cathedral work crews, under the able foremanship of Jeremy Bradley, are every day helping our parishioners tear out soaked carpet and drywall and moving belongings to safer places. Additionally, we have matched parishioners who are displaced from their homes in temporary housing with parishioners who have a garage apartment or available guest room.

We have also compiled a list of parish attorneys, who have graciously offered their knowledge *pro bono* to assist those dealing with the arcane language of FEMA or insurance.

We've made plans for The Beacon temporarily to expand its mission, to offer service seven days a week rather than five, and to serve three meals per day rather than one. This will, by the way, require our parishioners—those of us here in this room—to step forward and volunteer, especially Tuesdays and Wednesdays, which are days The Beacon is normally closed. Register to volunteer on The Beacon's web site, www.beaconhomeless.org.

And, we're working far beyond our parish boundaries. At Bishop Doyle's request, the Cathedral has taken the lead in organizing a network of Episcopal parishes through-out the city, including St. Martin's, St. John the Divine, Palmer, St. Mark's, Trinity, St. Francis, and Holy Spirit, to connect aid with needs across the city in the most efficient and effective way. Our CUSE (Cathedral Urban Service Experience) director, Christy Orman, has been named Hurricane Relief Administrator for this effort. The results of this work will have an enormous long-term impact on Houston's recovery.

In the wake of disaster, beyond the wilderness, when everything is stripped bare, the God whom fire cannot consume and water cannot drown comes to us and says, *I will send you.* God is calling now—us, this Cathedral, this community of disciples—and God does not send us alone. We are Christ Church together, and we will see the dawn.

10

The Ten Commandments

EXODUS 20:1-7

MARCH 4, 2018

PERHAPS MORE THAN ANY OTHER PORTION of Holy Scripture, the Ten Commandments are misused as a tool for secular ideological ends. Utilizing the Bible in this way is an error and not an act of fidelity to God's Word. Returning to Karl Barth's dictum discussed in the introduction, first we must know the scriptures deeply and well. Then, and only then, can the scriptures become for us a lens by which to interpret and respond to the world.

Many of a certain generation will remember the scene from the Mel Brooks film *History of the World: Part I*, when Moses stands atop Mount Sinai looking down upon the Hebrews with three large stone tablets balanced precariously in his hands. Moses (played by Brooks himself, of course) says to the Israelites, "Oh, hear me! All pay heed! The Lord, the Lord Jehovah, has given unto you these fifteen—" At which point Moses drops one of the three tablets, and it shatters. He pauses sheepishly, mumbles "Oy," and then says, "Ten! *Ten* commandments for all to obey!"

In 2006, Georgia Congressman Lynn Westmoreland sponsored a bill declaring that the Ten Commandments are "fundamental principles" and "the cornerstone of a just and fair society." Congressman Westmoreland's bill would also have required that the Ten Commandments be prominently displayed in the US Capitol Building.[1] In an interview, Westmoreland explained, "Well, the Ten Commandments is not a bad thing for people to understand and respect. Where better could you have something like that than a judicial building or a courthouse?"

Whether or not one agrees with the placement of religious monuments on public property, surely most people would agree with the congressman's sentiment about understanding and respecting such a foundational part of our religious and cultural tradition. So far, so good.

But then the interviewer asked the obvious follow-up: "What are the Ten Commandments? Can you name them all?"

For just a split-second, Congressman Westmoreland looked stupefied, as if it never occurred to him that the interview might take such a turn. He then responded, "What are all of them? You want me to name them *all?*" (A pregnant pause.) "Don't murder; don't lie; don't steal… Um…I can't name them all."[2]

The point is that the Ten Commandments, like so much else in religious life in different eras and at different places, have become a fetish, a symbol of something that bears very little relationship to the content of the commandments themselves. If we take the good Congressman at his word that the Ten Commandments are a cornerstone of a just and fair society and that they deserve our understanding and respect, then the first step is not to chisel them in marble and set them on the courthouse lawn but to *know what they say* and, with God's help, follow them.

So, let's look with attention and care at the Ten Commandments. We'll consider what they actually say and why they might matter in our lives.

At the outset, it is important to remember the context in which God issues these commandments. The Israelites have just been redeemed from bondage in Egypt. After many generations of slavery, they are free; yet they have no idea what it looks like to live as free people who serve under no one's arbitrary yoke. God grants the Ten Commandments to the Israelites not as a stifling burden but as the broad, corralling boundaries within which the life of free people can be lived in mutuality, respect, and joy. The commandments intend to provide for us the same.

We'll save the first three commandments for last, and this re-ordering will make sense when we return to commandments one-three. The fourth commandment is "Remember the sabbath day, and keep it holy." Throughout most of human history, when labor was grinding, back-breaking, and incessant, the sabbath day was, literally, life-saving. It gave the body time to heal and restore its energy. In today's world the sabbath is equally crucial. We are workaholics. With email, cell phones, and social media, our work creeps into every area of our lives, including the dinner table and bedroom. And this phenomenon occurs not only in our paid labor. Even our recreation increasingly has a job-like quality to it (think: kids' sports). In every facet of our lives, we want to accomplish, achieve, and do more. Consequently, we are perpetually fatigued: physically, psychologically, and emotionally. We are weary, but we do not rest. God understands our human need, and God commands us to observe sabbath. Imagine how different our lives would be if, for twenty-four hours a week, we shed the need to *do* and concentrated on *being:* being present to ourselves, to God, and to those we love. If nothing else, our blood pressure would benefit from the change.

The fifth commandment is "Honor your father and mother." In our psychological age, this one can trip us up because, frankly, some among us endured bad fathers and mothers. Healing psychologically from abuse can be a lifelong effort. But even for such people, the importance of the fifth commandment is the reminder that none of us is entirely self-made. Where we love, we have learned from someone to love. Where we have advantage, we have benefitted from someone who sacrificed to grant us that advantage. It is our sacred responsibility to maintain a posture of remembrance and response to the generation from which we have sprung: not to ignore its faults and flaws but to nevertheless acknowledge our gratitude by granting it grace.

The behavioral commandments come next. They are basic and unassailable, which is exactly why humanity has always been mystified at its inability to keep them!

The breadth of the sixth commandment—"Do not murder"—is a topic of endless theological debate. Some believe it intends a blanket prohibition against all killing;

others believe it is more specific, referring to unlawful killing while acknowledging that in our broken world there are circumstances of justice that require the taking of a life by appropriate authorities. In either case, the commandment decrees that life belongs to God and not us, that life—all life, not only the lives of those we love—is to be treated with awe and reverence.

The seventh commandment, "Do not commit adultery," could not be clearer. A priest once said to me, "Half the world's problems would be solved if people would not have sexual relations with people to whom other people are married." Let that sink in for a moment before we move on.

The eighth commandment, "Do not steal," means do not take as your own those things that are not yours, or are not yours entirely. In our world, where resources are sometimes scarce, this is doubly important. Failure to share those things we rightly hold in common is a form of theft, as surely as my pick-pocketing your wallet is theft.

The tenth commandment, "Do not covet your neighbor's house," concerns "the destructive power of desire."[3] Though it comes later in the list, it logically precedes "Do not steal." If one indulges a covetousness for what belongs to another, then over time one will rationalize taking that thing by any means available, lawful or unlawful.

Sandwiched between these two commandments is the ninth, against bearing false witness. This does refer to general falsehoods. It refers to claiming as true a depiction of reality one knows to be false. The commandment prohibits falsely marring another's reputation, either in malice or ignorance. It condemns distorting the truth to prop up one's ideology. I wish Congressman Westmoreland and all his colleagues on both sides of the aisle would learn this commandment most of all.

The Ten Commandments begin with the most important three, which are prioritized even before the laws against murder and theft. The commandments begin with God saying, "You shall have no other gods before me. You shall not make for yourself an idol. You shall not make wrongful use of the name of the Lord your God." These three commands are the backdrop of the other seven. They tell us that we must not consider God peripherally, casually, or flippantly. We must not use God or God's name as a tool, a means to our own ends. The theologian Paul Tillich famously said that our god is that in which we place our ultimate concern. We could each ask ourselves, "What is my god? To what do I give my greatest attention, energy, money? What is my ultimate concern in my daily life?" If the answer is anything but the God of love, then our lives are askew. All of the other commandments will then be more difficult to keep, because love is in not the center, the core from which all our living extends.

To live as a free people, today as in ancient Israel, means to live attentive to, grounded by, and centered in the God of love. When we live this way, we will care for ourselves with rest, we will respect those from whom we've come, we will honor the vows to our loved ones, we will revere life, we will be satisfied with enough in life, and we will speak truth to ourselves and others. Living so is not bondage; it is freedom. It is the gift to us from the God of love and the invitation to live our lives in God.

11

Without Love, All Is Lost

1 JOHN 4:8.

APRIL 22, 2018

FIRST LADY BARBARA BUSH, wife of 41st President of the United States George H.W. Bush, died on April 17, 2018, at age 92. Reminiscences of Mrs. Bush emphasized her gentility and civility, as well as her empathy for others. During her public life, Mrs. Bush worked tirelessly to alleviate illiteracy. She also extended care and understanding toward those with AIDS during a time when many AIDS patients were shunned by society.

On Monday I wrote a sermon. I drafted it, let it sit overnight, worked on it some more, and then had my wife, Jill, read it. She gave it the clergy-spouse seal of approval, so I was ready for today. It was a pretty good sermon. When it was neatly printed and placed in the center of my desk, I was relieved, as I always am. (I'm fastidious like that.) But I'm not preaching that sermon. Late in the week I deep-sixed it in the recycle bin. I'm preaching something different.

Usually, I preach on the Gospel. Occasionally, I preach on the Old Testament text. Almost never do I preach on the Epistle. At three of our four English-language services on Sunday, most weeks we don't even read the Epistle. But last Sunday afternoon, when I read today's propers for the first time, I dutifully read the Epistle, and as the week wore on, it tightened its grip on me and wouldn't let go.

And then, on Tuesday evening Barbara Bush died. I only met Mrs. Bush once, and then only in passing. Her death ought not to have affected me beyond being a notable headline. Perhaps it was because so many broadcasters referred to Mrs. Bush as "America's Mom." I'm not sure. Regardless, as I pondered her gentility, her civility, her empathy for those around her, I began to lament. The loss of Barbara Bush strikes me, if you'll allow a crude analogy, the way that the loss of a white rhinoceros does: There are too few of them remaining, and we can't afford to lose another.

I don't mean to idealize Mrs. Bush unrealistically. I am told that she could be a pistol in private. My deeper lament is for the state of our culture, which the loss of Mrs. Bush accentuated for me. It seems to me that, in our culture, our capacity for empathy is failing us.

I am not alone in my lament. Gary Olson, author of *Empathy Imperiled: Capitalism, Culture, and the Brain,* says that our society increasingly "displays an anesthetized conscience towards the suffering of others."[1] Olson goes on to say that we hear the cries of those in all sorts of need around us, but our "moral sound waves are muted as they pass through powerful cultural baffles."[2]

That resonates with me. At every turn in our culture, it seems, something discourages empathy. Politics is now so divisive, with a vanishing sense of the common good. Officials elected to represent a constituency increasingly refuse to receive comments or concerns from constituents not of their political party, as if they only represent those who voted for them.

Sarcasm—vicious, biting sarcasm—is the *lingua franca* of the day, from politicians, late night television hosts, and even colleagues at the water cooler. Increasingly, people will malign anyone, irrespective of the cost to that person, as if zingers score some sort of cosmic points.

The author Peter Bazalgette points to the Internet's lack of empathy as the drain down which our capacity for empathy is spiraling. Bazalgette says, "If you take the average working environment now, you spend most of your time not talking to people or even phoning them but sending them an email. Without facial expressions or tone of voice, you're not aware of the impact of words. [We] see this with cyber bullying and revenge porn, [where people] don't see the victim of [their] bad behavior."[3]

Gary Olson might agree that the Internet is a contributor, but he believes the problem is much more pervasive. Olson says, "We [have] come to view our 'selves,' our identities, as based primarily on market values, especially 'Only care about yourself and a few persons close to you.' One advances in society via rugged self-reliance, and individuals are basically hypercompetitive, perpetual consumers."[4]

Olson may be right. I remember a time when the media used to refer to the American public as "citizens," whereas now that term has been completely supplanted by "consumers." We approach the world by what use it is to us, and too often the real and sensitive lives of other people are barriers to be avoided or overcome, not empathized with.

What *is* empathy? I know of no better definition than Harper Lee's, placed on the lips of Atticus Finch and spoken to Scout in *To Kill A Mockingbird*. Atticus says to his young daughter, "You never really understand a person until you consider things from his point of view... Until you climb into his skin and walk around in it."[5]

When was the last time many of us really, truly did that? Empathy is more than charity or sympathy. Empathy is more than doing a kindness. Empathy is being vulnerable enough to see the world through the eyes—the experience—of another. Empathy is an act of love.

And that's why today's Epistle lesson grabbed hold of me this week and would not let me go. Today we read from the First Letter of John, which reveals to us a few verses after today's reading that "God is love."[6]

Note John's language carefully. John does *not* say that God *loves*. Loving is not a thing God *does*, like brushing God's teeth or mowing the grass. John says that God *is* love. That is who and what God is *in God's very nature*. God's character is love. God's passion is love. God's commitment to the world is love. And God carried out the supreme act of empathy when God, literally, took Atticus Finch's advice. As Jesus, God climbed into our skin and walked around in it. God experienced the world as we do, with our confusion, our vulnerability, and our pain. Today John says, "We know love by this, that [Jesus] laid down his life for us."

God's empathy for us becomes our model and calling—and not only because the world needs it. Remember,

God himself is love, and 1 John tells us that the ways we meet God, and know God, and deeply encounter God are through our acts of empathy and love. When we love, God flows through us. John asks, "How does God's love abide in anyone who has the world's goods and sees a brother or sister in need and yet refuses help? Little children, let us love, not [only] in word or speech, but in truth and action."

Why, so often, are we unable to do this? Why are we susceptible to allowing the anonymity of the Internet or the consumerism of our culture to create barriers between us and our fellow human beings? David Niose, who blogs for *Psychology Today*, believes our lack of empathy has its roots in fear.[7] We are fearful of the world's cruelty and of the things we have being taken away from us. The irony is, of course, that our fear creates the very cruelty of which we are afraid. The irony is that without empathy, without the capacity to love our fellow human beings, we lose our relationships with them and we lose, by definition, our relationship with the God who is love.

In the novel *Beneath a Scarlet Sky*, the priest Father Re says to Pino, a teenager who is afraid to help Italian Jews escape to Switzerland over the Alps, "We can't stop loving our fellow man, Pino, because we're frightened. If we lose love, all is lost."[8]

Earlier in 1 John, John says, "We pass from death to life because we love one another."[9] Those are the truest words I know. If we lose love, all is lost. So let us go from this place with the willingness to climb into one another's skin, to see through one another's eyes, and to allow the God who is greater than our hearts to swell those hearts with empathy and love.

Christian & American

12

Of Liberty,
Christian and American

MATTHEW 11:16-19, 25-30

SUNDAY, JULY 6, 2014

Not like the brazen giant of Greek fame,
With conquering limbs astride from land to land;
Here at our sea-washed, sunset gates shall stand
A mighty woman with a torch, whose flame
Is the imprisoned lightning, and her name
Mother of Exiles. From her beacon-hand
Glows world-wide welcome; her mild eyes command
The air-bridged harbor that twin cities frame.
"Keep, ancient lands, your storied pomp!" cries she
With silent lips. "Give me your tired, your poor,
Your huddled masses yearning to breathe free,
The wretched refuse of your teeming shore.
Send these, the homeless, tempest-tossed to me,
I lift my lamp beside the golden door!

Do you know those words? I suspect you recall, as I did, two lines a little more than halfway through the poem: "Give me your tired, your poor, your huddled masses yearning to breathe free." The poem is "New Colossus," penned by Jewish poet Emma Lazarus in 1883. Lazarus wrote and donated the sonnet to a fundraiser for the pedestal of the Statue of Liberty, which would be dedicated along with the statue itself three years later, in 1886. "New Colossus" is now inscribed on a bronze plaque at the base of that same pedestal.

In today's Gospel reading from Matthew, Jesus says, "Come to me, all you that are weary and heavy laden, and I will give you rest." We read these words each week in the Holy Eucharist, Rite I. Liturgically they are called, in fact, the "comfortable words," and they do, indeed, provide us comfort.

Jesus's words are strikingly like those of Emma Lazarus' poem, and there is serendipity—or Providence—in their convergence on Independence Day weekend. During this time of year when Americans tend to become preoccupied with the relationship of our nationhood to our faith, the similarity of these sentiments bears further consideration. What do Jesus's words mean? And what about the words of "New Colossus?"

Jesus's invitation to holy comfort and rest come at the end of a longer speech, which actually begins not with solace but with indictment. Jesus is speaking to people who want to be spoon-fed salvation. He reminds them that he and John the Baptist have each come proclaiming God: John in ominous and austere tones, and Jesus himself in joy. But neither message has made a dent in today's audience. They have responded neither to carrot nor stick. Jesus compares the gathered crowd to children, saying, "We played the flute for you, and you did not dance. Then we wailed, and you did not mourn."

Why hasn't this crowd responded to the Gospel? Well, both John the Baptist's and Jesus's messages have included a required commitment to God, a dedication to a transformed way of life, and that's more than the people want to hear. They want comfort without struggle. They want rest without exertion. They want new life, but they want to keep their old ways of living, too. They're like us, in other words.

But there is no way around the commitment if we want to receive the comfort. Jesus, today's Gospel says, is the very Wisdom of God. More than a wise teacher, Jesus is God's heart and mind, and the words of Jesus are the truth of God. And that spoken truth is that receiving the refuge and rest of God's love necessarily includes taking on the burden, shackling ourselves with the yoke of commitment to God.

The irony, of course, is that God's very yoke is liberty! To take on the burden of God's Gospel is also to cast off the heavy weights, like anvils on the shoulders, with which we trudge through the world. We, like the crowd, have walked through the world with those weights for so long, we've come to mistake our slumped shoulders for good posture. Our anxiety, self-doubt, striving, loathing, fear: God has nothing to do with these. They are worldly burdens, not burdens God casts upon us, but we come to define ourselves by them. They become the crutches on which we prop ourselves, and heavy as they are we can scarcely imagine being without them.

Even so, Jesus calls out God's truth, "Take my yoke upon you, and learn from me; for I am gentle and humble in heart, and you will find rest for your souls. For my yoke is easy, and my burden is light."

Jesus's is the yoke of liberty *from* anxiety, from self-doubt, from loathing, from fear. It is the *yoke of love,* under which we learn to love and accept ourselves, and under which we extend grace and dignity to those around us. Do you see how this liberty requires commitment? Do you see the yoke involved in doing these things, in self-acceptance and love of neighbor?

That is what Jesus's words mean this morning. What of Emma Lazarus' words? Well, there is more discretion there. Hers are not the words of God's Wisdom, and so their truth is malleable. Each generation must define what is meant by our nation's liberty. Each generation must decide for what Lady Liberty stands.

Liberty today tends, in our common consciousness, to stand for freedom from all constraints, freedom from any and all fetters placed upon us. We believe we enjoy the most liberty when we are free to do whatever, whenever and however we choose. I'll admit that this is a kind of liberty, to be sure, but it is the kind St. Augustine calls *libertas minor,* or small freedom.[1] Our desire that others leave us be and not tell us what we must do is rooted in our anxiety and our fear. It is nothing more, Augustine suggests, than the kind of liberty shared by wild animals.

And, as any careful student of our nation's founding generation knows, it is not the liberty they had in mind, nor is it the liberty transparently embodied in the original meaning of Emma Lazarus' words at the Statue of Liberty.

St. Augustine also speaks of *libertas major*, the big free-dom, which is the uniquely human liberty to submit one-self freely to an ideal—to a spirit—to give oneself over to something larger than one's own animal instincts, wants, and needs.[2] It is the liberty that includes a yoke: a commit-ment to subsume one's own individual freedoms within a cause that is of greater value than one's personal concerns. The founding generation didn't say to their brothers and sisters, "Leave me alone; I'm free and you can't tell me what to do!" They gave of their intellects, their fortunes, their comfort, and often their very lives in support of the big freedom, for the conviction that this is a new land in a New World, for the ideal that all here are of worth and merit human dignity and care.

In that way Emma Lazarus' words are very like the words of Jesus. And, it turns out, the ideals behind her sonnet are akin to the Wisdom of God. What is American liberty, according to the inscription at the Statue of Liberty?

American liberty is *not*, ultimately, the demand that no one tell me what to do. American liberty *is*, ultimately, the freedom to cast off the weight of what the Old World says is true about me, about my worth and place in society. American liberty is to shed those anxieties and fears. And, it is to commit myself, body and soul, to the embrace of the hurting, the tempest-tossed, the discarded, that they, too, might taste the liberty I enjoy; that their lives, too, might then be committed to the liberty of all.

A few months ago I received a mass email (as I do ev-ery year) that encouraged everyone who attended a pub-lic high school graduation this spring spontaneously to stand and recite the Lord's Prayer. Such would, the email's author claimed, demonstrate that we are a religious people, a Christian nation at heart. I don't buy that. I love the Lord's Prayer. Indeed, I suspect I pray it more often than most people. But rather than demonstrating that a gymnasium or stadium-full of people merely know the words, I'm more interested in us taking on the yoke of laboring to ensure that God's will is done on earth as it is in heaven, that all are given this day their daily bread, that the kingdom of liberty and love is realized as fully as possible on this side of the veil.

Still, on this weekend of the nation's two hundred and thirty-eighth birthday, the Statue of Liberty stands as faithful sentry in New York Harbor, as guardian of all we, as a nation, hold to be true. She, with mild eyes and liberty's flame, rises above those words that embody the very best of what we, as a nation, hope and intend to be. She stands for freedom, freedom for the dignity of all people, liberty for the tempest-tossed and the lonely. She is a beacon for this freedom. I pray we will be, too.

13

To Be a Patriot

MARK 6:1-13

JULY 5, 2016

FROM THAT NIGHT ON, he knew they'd kill him. He had come home a day after having been arrested, intimidated, and thrown in jail for a trumped-up traffic violation. His wife and baby daughter were in bed. It was midnight, and he sat alone at the kitchen table. The phone rang, and when he answered it a voice on the other end of the line vomited every epithet imaginable, putting particular emphasis on the N-word. Then the voice said, "We've taken everything from you we want. Before next week you'll be sorry you ever came to Montgomery."

And Martin Luther King Jr. knew. He didn't know if it would be the next day, the next week, or next year, but he knew just as certainly as if an Old Testament prophet had predicted it eons ago that they would kill him if he would not be silent.

That night, Martin Luther King was doubting and afraid. He thought of his wife and daughter and the danger to which he'd exposed them. He felt himself begin to falter under the weight of his conviction.

In today's reading from Mark, Jesus comes home. When last Jesus left Nazareth, he was a construction worker, a day laborer, which is what "carpenter" most likely means in the biblical context, who'd wandered south to check out his crazy cousin John baptizing in the River Jordan. The good folk of Nazareth haven't seen him since, but they've received increasingly strange reports by those who travel through town. If the reports weren't so frequent, they'd be dismissed as so many jokes. First, citizens hear this Jesus—a poor, lower-class boy born in questionable circumstances—is preaching in the countryside as if he knows God. That's bad enough.

But then reports waft in that with Jesus the mentally ill have been soothed. The sick have been healed. Those whose lives are paralyzed have found the strength to walk, to move forward with new hope and promise. Worst of all, as Jesus's power has grown, his message has become threatening to some. He has spoken of the Way that leads to the kingdom of God, and however one tries to interpret it, it is a way that brings discomfort to those who are comfortable as it raises up those whom the world has cast low.

Today, unannounced, Jesus walks back into Nazareth, his hometown. The Greek word for hometown used in Mark is *patris*, which is the same root from which we get the terms patriot and patriotism. That's interesting, isn't it? That the Lectionary would posit this text on this of all weekends, as our eyes still glimmer in the afterglow of last night's fireworks, with our stomachs still comfortably full of Independence Day fare, suggests to me what might be called in today's parlance a "God moment."

On Independence Day weekend, it is surely fair to ask, "What *is* patriotism?" At its root, as in Mark today, to be a patriot is simply to be from the *patris*, nothing more or less than to be a member of some organized political entity: a city, a state, or a nation. But we know from the emotions that welled in us as last night's sky was lit by starbursts that, for us, patriotism is also more than this. Indeed, the second verse of "America the Beautiful" says, "O beautiful for heroes proved in liberating strife."

Patriotism, then, is tied to liberty. But what is liberty? The easiest answer might be that liberty is freedom from any and all fetters placed upon us. We enjoy the most liberty in this sense when we are free to do whatever, whenever and however we choose. But that is, at root, a selfish definition, and it doesn't fit with the verse just quoted, about those "who more than self their country loved." The heroes of Katherine Lee Bate's blessed hymn were focused not on their own individualistic selves, but on something larger than themselves. What was it? The hymn reminds us: They sacrificed their very lives to free their brothers and sisters from strife. This was the liberty they cherished, for which they lived and died: to raise up the one next to them, to ensure his liberty, or hers.

The ideal of this great *patris* in which we are blessed to live was penned by Thomas Jefferson two and a half centuries ago: "We hold these truths to be self-evident: that all men are created equal, that they are endowed by their Creator with certain unalienable rights." And patriots are those who give themselves to this ideal of the *patris*, who are willing to sacrifice even life, if necessary, to ensure that this equality and these rights are freely enjoyed by all.

As a sidebar, it's important to note that patriotism differs from nationalism. Nationalism extols the existence of the state for its own sake. The state is seen as the collective embodiment of power, strength, and security. The core of one's being becomes the state—not its virtues or ideals but the mere fact of it. The state becomes a fetish and an idol on which the nationalist hangs his hopes, and the nationalist obstinately refuses to acknowledge when the state has become an impediment to liberty rather than its defender. Beware nationalism. Beware when we hear it from our politicians, and doubly beware when we hear it from our preachers.

Not so, patriotism. Rather than giving his heart to the mere fact of the *patris*, the patriot gives his heart to the best that the *patris* stands for, and the patriot does this even in the face of fear, challenge, ridicule, and assault by those who claim patriotism but have lost an understanding of what liberty really means.

We see, then, in Mark that Jesus is the patriot. He enters the *patris* of his hometown as the one who embodies, come what may, God's hope for Israel, the liberty that is the kingdom of God. But we must pay attention to the character of this liberty. It is a liberty in which all the lonely and the lost are found; those with blinded eyes—and those with blinded hearts—are given sight; those who have been pushed to the bottom of society and walked upon are raised up in love.

The citizens of Nazareth want nothing to do with this patriot Jesus. His liberty doesn't strike them as good news. It sounds threatening to their well-being. It sounds as if it might require something of them, some sort of cataclysmic change in the way they see the world, like fireworks lighting up a darkened night sky. And so they ridicule Jesus. They spread rumors that he has no father. They threaten him. In Luke's account they actually manhandle Jesus and try to throw him off a cliff in order to shut him up. They'll fail in that attempt, and he won't be silenced, but Jesus also knows the cost of his patriotism will eventually be his death. Self-sacrifice is the price he'll pay for his commitment to the liberty of God.

In the past two weeks, this nation has changed mightily. Things tragic, joyous, and challenging all occurred: the shootings at Emanuel AME Church in Charleston, the Supreme Court's ruling on same-sex marriage, the historic changes wrought at our own General Convention. And now we come to the nation's birthday celebration.

Often on Independence Day weekend, the question arises whether the United States is a Christian nation. People with varying stakes in the answer to this question address it in different ways. I would respond by asking about the character of our patriotism. What does it look like? It seems to me that the degree to which we are both faithful Christians and good patriots is perhaps best discerned by the degree to which our American patriotism also looks like the patriotism of Jesus, the degree to which we pursue *his* liberty in our private and public lives, in our hearts and in society, and the degree to which we are committed to that liberty, even in the midst of ridicule and danger.

In other words, for those of use who claim to be both Christian and American, our patriotism is measured by whether or not we are working toward a day in which the kingdom of God envisioned by Jesus is witnessed in the nation around us. According to that yardstick, in our responses to the issues facing us these days, how patriotic are we?

Real patriotism was surely evident in the tortured prayer of that twenty-seven-year-old preacher in Montgomery who understood better than most what it looks like to champion the kingdom of God in the *patris*. That night Martin Luther King prayed, "Lord…I'm weak now; I'm faltering; I'm losing my courage."

And Jesus Christ responded, "Martin, stand up. Take courage. And I will be with you to the end of the world." And King stood as a patriot, even at the cost of his own life.

We remember again this weekend the birth of a nation unlike any other, one founded not through a desire for power but through a passion for liberty. May liberty be *our* passion, through which we commit ourselves to God's vision for this and every land. It is a vision in which aching hearts stand not alone, hungry children are fed, and lost souls are found; where those of us born of plenty freely give of our lives in order that all God's children may know love and joy. May that vision dazzle us like fireworks in the sky, so that we commit ourselves to it against every challenge—including self-sacrifice if necessary—and so that we stand up and take courage wherever God leads us.

14

Birth: A Reflection for Independence Day

JULY 2, 2017

SEVENTEEN YEARS AGO ON JULY 2, my wife was due to give birth. We were in Jackson, Tennessee; it was blazing hot; and Jill was ready to burst. We walked our neighborhood incessantly, hoping to entice and coax our firstborn child to make his entrance into the world. He was having nothing of it. Day after day, Jill and I walked. Day after day, the baby obstinately stayed put.

Of course, our attention had been attuned to this child for a very long time, even longer than the nine months he had been forming in the womb. For the previous five years of our marriage, Jill and I had talked about the child we hoped, one day, to have. We had debated the values we would seek to instill in him. We had negotiated how we would plan for his future. We had dreamed of what impact he might make upon the world.

A full week after the due date, on July 7, the baby still offered no sign of his appearing, and our obstetrician decided to induce labor. We entered the hospital early that morning, Jill was given a healthy dose of Pitocin, and we expected that soon we'd have a cooing, gurgling baby. July 7 passed in discomfort but with no child. Twenty-four hours turned into thirty-six before Jill's body and the baby showed any inclination to give birth. When things finally did start to happen, the baby became lodged in the birth canal, and there he stayed for what seemed like forever. Finally, his heart rate fell precipitously; and, with such speed that I didn't realize what was happening, the doctor used forceps to retrieve our son and pull him, seemingly against his will, into the world.

The baby didn't cry. He was limp and lethargic. Looks of concern spread across the faces in the room. A special care nurse was summoned. An oxygen bag was applied. And I, a new and first-time father, stood to the side paralyzed, wondering if this event would end badly, if the plans we'd made for nine months, or the hopes we'd carried for five years, would leave us bereft.

It is impossible for me to celebrate my son's birthday without dwelling upon, and sometimes losing myself within, the memory of his birth. I daresay my gratitude to God is deepened because, for a moment, I teetered on the very edge of loss. I also carry a potent sense of the precariousness of the project that is my son. Each of his birthdays, like the day of his actual birth, is a moment filled with hope, and anticipation, and apprehension for what the coming year may bring. All that preparation and planning that began five years before he entered the world is still operative.

My son's birthday is the same week as Independence Day. Sometimes the two events get muddled in my thinking. I love them both, my son and the United States. The coincidence of these auspicious dates also reminds me that Independence Day is a birthday, the anniversary observance of the entrance into the world of something uniquely new.

For years before our nation's birth, there were those who debated the values this new thing would embody. They planned for its arrival. They imagined the impact it would have on the world. What was born was not solely, or even primarily, the legal entity of a nation, but rather an *idea*. And though the Founders' understanding of God was not, on the whole, orthodox, the idea gestated by them was commensurate with the Gospel. The idea was that "all men are created equal, that they are endowed by their Creator with certain unalienable Rights, [and] that among these are Life, Liberty, and the pursuit of Happiness." It is an idea about shared human dignity and worth, about the commonweal of which we are all a part, about a city on a hill rather than a society in which any must crawl in the gutter.

The birth was announced on July 4, 1776, but the announcement came at the beginning, rather than the end, of the birthing process. Labor turned out to be painful, lengthy, and precarious. It began at Lexington and Concord, and it endured through Appomattox, Normandy's beaches, the Edmund Pettus Bridge, and the Twin Towers. In truth, it continues today. There were times when the idea being birthed seemed stuck, when its heartbeat seemed to fade, when Americans felt paralyzed as events swirled around them, and in their fear didn't know how to act—or, worse yet, acted badly.

At such times, they might've given up on the idea. We still might. The laboring process faces us anew in every generation. We might decide that the idea isn't what's valuable, that it doesn't matter, that we can abandon labor, leaving the idea half-birthed, and live as Americans anyway.

But we cannot do these things, any more than I could have walked out of the labor and delivery room seventeen years ago. My son was being born. There was nothing in this world more valuable or precious. All the planning, all the passion, all the love that brought us to that day hinged on the birth of that child. Whatever happened next, life would never be the same.

And the same is true of the United States. We are only American to the extent that our lives are dedicated wholly to the birth, health, and growth of a land marked by liberty for all. It is the land we bequeath to our flesh and blood children. It is the land that continues to be the iconic hope of the rest of the world. If we ever walk away from birthing the *idea* of the United States, then it will be stillborn; and, in spirit at least, this great nation will cease to be.

When my son was in peril in the moments after his birth, our saving grace was the doctor, who all the while tended to Jill and offered us both confident words of encouragement and resolve. In moments of our nation's peril, sages and prophets have emerged who do the same. In December 1862, a year and a half after the outbreak of the Civil War and three months after the Battle of

Antietam, which is still the bloodiest day in American history, Abraham Lincoln addressed Congress. He spoke to encourage the emancipation of Southern slaves, but his words are timeless. They apply equally to any moment in our nation's history when the laboring process is distressed, when we Americans allow our divisions to paralyze us.

At the end of his speech, Lincoln considered his generation's legacy with both warning and hope. Hear his words, but allow them to speak to us.

> We cannot escape history. We...will be remembered in spite of ourselves. No personal significance, or insignificance, can spare one or another of us. The fiery trial through which we pass, will light us down, in honor or dishonor, to the latest generation. We say we are for the [United States]. The world will not forget that we say this. We...hold the power, and bear the responsibility...We shall nobly save, or meanly lose, the last best hope of earth...The way is plain, peaceful, generous, just—a way which, if followed, the world will forever applaud, and God must forever bless.[2]

As I write, my almost-seventeen-year-old son is on his way home from Costa Rica with fifteen of his fellow parishioners, where they have served as the hands and feet of Christ for people in grave need. All that planning, all that apprehension, all that hope...I am, this day, a proud father. I love my son.

I also love the idea of the United States, for which so many before us have given their hearts, their hopes, and their lives. With one another, and for those who look to us in hope across this globe, I pray that we will follow the way that is peaceful, generous, and just. If we do, then God will, indeed, forever bless.

Open Questions

I Own Guns, and I Believe in Gun Control

AUGUST 29, 2015

IN 2014, the Federal Bureau of Investigation reported that mass shootings in the United States almost tripled within the span of a half-decade.[1] This statistic was punctuated by mass shootings of horrific scope, including the shooting at Sandy Hook Elementary School on December 14, 2012 in Newtown, Connecticut, in which twenty children and six adults were murdered.

I own guns. I am a bird hunter, and I own shotguns for that purpose. I also own a single-action, six-shot revolver loaded with shotshells as protection against poisonous snakes on my family's small piece of land in the country, where copperheads are as common as mosquitoes. Before I was a teenager, my father taught me to shoot guns responsibly. I am teaching my kids to do the same.

I am also, like so many, appalled at the gun violence endemic in our country, violence amplified this past week by the on-air murder of two journalists, Alison Parker and Adam Ward, outside my former hometown of Roanoke, Virginia, and the gas-station assassination of a deputy sheriff, Darren Goforth, in my present hometown of Houston, Texas. These horrific events come on the heels of this summer's murders at Mother Emanuel AME Church in Charleston, South Carolina, that followed a year of high-profile shootings of unarmed black men and years of school shootings that extend all the way back to the March 1998 Westside Elementary School shooting in Northeast Arkansas, a half hour from the community of my birth.

In a culture increasingly marked by histrionic rhetoric on virtually every topic of concern to the commonweal, no topics have greater tangible or numeric impact—and no topics incite greater hysteria—than gun violence and gun control.

Last week, *New York Times* columnist Nicholas Kristoff published a column[2] in which he offered several points of fact (points later verified by the web site Politifact.com). These include:

- More Americans die by gun violence every six months than have died in the last twenty-five years in every terrorist attack and in the wars in Afghanistan and Iraq combined.
- More Americans have died from guns in the United States since 1968 than on all the battlefields of all the wars in American history.
- American children are fourteen times as likely to die from guns as children in other developed countries.

Additionally, in 2013 ABC News provided comparative statistics for gun deaths in the United States versus other developed countries. Per 100,000 people, Great Britain suffers .25 deaths by gun violence annually. Australia experiences 1.4 deaths by gun violence. The United States tops the lists—beating even South Africa—with a staggering 10.2 deaths per 100,000 people. We have a problem, and it's time we acknowledged as much.

Those opposed to any gun control claim that guns, as inanimate objects, don't kill people. If one maintains that logic, then neither do automobiles kill people. And yet we regulate automobiles so law-abiding citizens are able to utilize them safely and not in ways that are likely to maim and kill. (As the father of a son approaching driving age, I'm particularly thankful for this regulation.)

"But driving is not a constitutional right, whereas gun ownership is," some will say. Indeed, in recent Supreme Court decisions *District of Columbia vs. Heller* and *McDonald vs. Chicago*, the Court ruled that under the Second Amendment United States citizens have just such a right to own handguns in addition to long guns such as shotguns and rifles. Though I am a priest and certainly not a legal scholar, I was raised by a mother who is an English teacher, and I would argue that in its recent rulings the Supreme Court failed the grammar lesson.

The Second Amendment reads: *"A well-regulated Militia, being necessary to the security of a free state, the right of the people to keep and bear arms, shall not be infringed."*

"A well-regulated Militia, being necessary to the security of a free state." The amendment's opening phrase is, in plain reading, integral to the meaning of the whole sentence. Blogger Mark Moe explains this better than I can:

> No less a constitutional authority than Supreme Court Chief Justice John Marshall [declares] that "it cannot be presumed that any clause in the constitution is intended to be without effect." *Thus, to call the first clause of the Second Amendment superfluous is to insult both Marshall and the framers.* The "absolute" clause construction of the Second Amendment was quite common at the time, and appears in many state constitutions and framing documents. The primary purpose in these constructions is to give the conditions under which the rest of the sentence is true or valid. As a prime example of the ablative absolute, the first clause of the Second Amendment may stand grammatically free, but serves semantically to modify or clarify the meaning of the rest of the sentence. The Framers were clearly familiar with the ablative absolute and used it not as rhetorical fluff or flourish, but as a way of clarifying intent, in this case clarifying that the right to bear arms is granted in the context and within the scope of establishing a militia. Nothing more, nothing less.[3]

Today, our militias consist of professional National Guards, not local Minute Men with muskets above the mantel. The right to bear arms is predicated, literally and grammatically, on a social institution that no longer exists. Be that as it may, the Supreme Court has ruled, and no jurisdiction may prohibit absolutely the ownership of handguns or long guns by citizens. And even if one could, a thoughtful and provocative essay by Jeffrey Goldberg in *The Atlantic* convinces me that American society is already so awash in guns that any outright prohibition would be impossible, even if it were advisable.[4]

I don't believe it is advisable. As I said at the outset, I am a gun owner who keeps and uses specific kinds of firearms for the intentions for which they were constructed. That said, on the topic of gun violence, statistical and anecdotal evidence coincide. We indeed have a festering societal problem, and as a minister of the Gospel of Jesus, the Prince of Peace, I say we have a moral problem. At least for those who follow the God of Jesus, a God whose vision for the world is that we "beat swords into ploughshares and spears into pruning hooks,"[5] the gun violence in our country is a symptom of soul sickness. Something must be done to stem the tide, and unfettered access to guns is no better solution than attempting to put out a fire with gasoline.

In its recent rulings, the Supreme Court affirms that gun regulation short of outright ban *is* permissible. Specifically, in the majority opinion of *District of Columbia vs. Heller*, Justice Scalia wrote:

> We also recognize another important limitation on the right to keep and carry arms. Miller said, as we have explained, that the sorts of weapons protected were those "in common use at the time." We think that limitation is fairly supported by the historical tradition of prohibiting the carrying of "dangerous and unusual weapons."

Justice Scalia adds: "Nothing in our opinion should be taken to cast doubt on...laws imposing conditions and qualifications on the commercial sale of arms."

Engaging in histrionics on either side of this debate is disingenuous and unhelpful. It is high time, I contend, that we dispassionately ask a basic question, seeking basic answers, and then develop policy and law based upon the answers:

Why do we wish to own guns?

Hunting, sporting, and home and/or personal protection seem to me to be the legitimate answers to the question. The guns I own are adequate to those uses. If I were a deer hunter, I would also own a deer rifle. What is unnecessary for any of these purposes is an assault rifle or a semi-automatic pistol with a high-capacity magazine. Such weapons are designed for the sole and express purpose of incapacitating many people quickly, which, lamentably in our broken world, is sometimes the responsibility of law enforcement and the military. Virtually never—even in a home-invasion situation—is it a circumstance legitimately faced by private citizens.

Personally, I favor prohibiting private ownership—not only sales of—assault rifles and other military-grade firearms, as well as high-capacity magazines for any firearm. It seems to me we should take Justice Scalia at his word and call these what they are: "dangerous and unusual weapons."

I favor a national firearm registry. Analogously, I have a constitutional right to vote, but I must register to do so.

I favor universal background checks and a return to the seven-day waiting period to purchase a handgun. Taking the long view, over a generation these serious, but not onerous, regulations might well shift both our culture's perspective on guns and actual gun violence statistics.

Before taking action, it would be very helpful to know what, if any, substantive positive effects on gun violence such regulations would have. I have little interest in feel-good palliatives that do no social good. Unfortunately, at this time, Congress will not fund gun violence prevention research at the Centers for Disease Control and Prevention. The best first step in approaching this vexing topic ratio-nally—in meeting our moral challenge—is to restore that funding. With reliable research, people of good will can be-gin working to prevent events such as Roanoke, Charleston, Sandy Hook, and Columbine from becoming daily experi-ence to which we are increasingly, despairingly numb.

Of Orlando and the Virtue of Embrace

JUNE 13, 2016

ON JUNE 12, 2016 AT 2 A.M., Omar Mateen walked into the Pulse LGBTQ nightclub in Orlando, Florida, and opened fire on more than three hundred patrons with a Sig Sauer MCX assault rifle and a Glock 9 mm semi-automatic pistol. Mateen killed forty-nine people and wounded more than fifty. At the time, the Pulse shooting was the deadliest mass shooting in American history. Tragically, it held that record for less than sixteen months, when it was surpassed by the Las Vegas mass shooting of October 1, 2017, which killed fifty-eight people.

Early yesterday morning, a twenty-nine-year-old man, full of hatred and armed to the teeth, walked into the Pulse nightclub in Orlando, Florida, and proceeded to murder fifty people and wound scores more. It is the most devastating mass shooting in American history. It specifically targeted the LGBTQ community.

In April of 1999, when two young men entered Columbine High School and began their massacre, I was twenty-six years old. I was young enough to remember vividly the experience of being in high school: in the library working on some project, in the cafeteria with friends. The familiarity of those spaces and my ability to imagine myself as a student at Columbine High School rendered that shooting intimately personal for me. It was a long time before I was able to think of Columbine without being overcome by emotion.

My life-long friends Elizabeth Bridges and Audra Hamilton, one gay and the other not, have both written with eloquence and passion in the past several hours about the way in which gay bars and night clubs are, for the LGBTQ community, places of sanctuary. In a Facebook post, Audra, who is not gay, speaks poignantly of the way in which she has always felt comfortable with friends in gay nightclubs. She muses why this is so and offers this: "I suspect it was…because the people who were there had fought so hard to create a place of acceptance for themselves…and I was a beneficiary of that space and that love. I felt free to be myself, because they did. And they welcomed me."

The complex role of gay bars and nightclubs in LGBTQ culture was news to me; I had been unaware. Though I minister to many gay and lesbian Christians, and though I am blessed to have gay and lesbian members of my family, I am unfamiliar with much of gay culture. And so, unlike Columbine, which resonated with familiar images and thus hit me viscerally, I am only just beginning to grasp the wound to the soul of the LGBTQ community caused by the massacre in Orlando, which may be more devastating even than the death toll.

This is, I believe, part of our collective challenge. We in the United States have striven to become a tolerant society. But mere tolerance doesn't breed familiarity, and without familiarity there is little chance for understanding. Tolerance is a passive virtue. It says, in essence, "I can abide your presence in proximity to me, but I do not want to know you."

I have plumbed the depths of the Gospels, and nowhere do I find Jesus exhibiting tolerance. Rather, Jesus embraces. Embrace is an active virtue, the preeminent Gospel virtue. Again and again, Jesus embraces the one who is outcast, who exists on the margins, who is maligned. Through his embrace, which comes in the forms both of physical contact and words of acceptance, Jesus declares that in God, there are no outcasts, there are no margins, and woe be it to anyone who maligns any one of God's blessed and beloved children.

With God's help, Christ Church Cathedral strives to be a Christian community of embrace. The Cathedral is, by definition, a sanctuary. Since at least the Middle Ages, churches-as-sanctuaries have been places where anyone, regardless of past, background, or way of life could find acceptance and refuge, where anyone could find embrace. But, even for churches, in times of apprehension and anxiety there is an impulse to give up the role of sanctuary in favor of the role of fortress: pulling up the drawbridge, flooding the moat, and manning the ramparts against the threatening other outside our walls.

We must not. We cannot. At a time when so many of those places people experience as sanctuaries in our world have been attacked—Pulse for the LGBTQ community in Orlando, Mother Emmanuel AME Church for the African-American community in Charleston, Sandy Hook Elementary for the precious children in Newtown, Connecticut, to name only a few—the witness of sacred sanctuaries that will not succumb to fear and will continue to embrace all God's children, come what may, has never been more important.

We are a sanctuary of the living Christ, into whose precincts are welcomed any and all who seek to know the God who is love. We are a community of arms open and ready to embrace. We must continue to be.

Who needs the embrace of Christ's whole church in these days? Surely, the Orlando community writ large, who are still reeling from disaster and will be for a long time. Surely, the LGBTQ community, who have been made to feel, as I felt after Columbine all those years ago, acutely vulnerable. And surely the mainstream Muslim community in this country, who must now contend not only with age-old and reciprocal mistrust between Christians and Muslims but also with the radicalized element within Islam, which is potent and real and whose very goal is to pit the rest of us against all our Muslim neighbors, the overwhelming majority of whom desire God's peace, just as we do.

Across social media, the question has been asked in various ways this past week, by people across social, ideological, and political spectra: "With whom do you stand?"

God willing, now as always, we stand with Jesus, because we believe Jesus is God Incarnate. And in this instance, I have no doubt where Jesus stands. Jesus stands in embrace of all of God's children who are afraid, who are suffering, and who are unsure what tomorrow will bring. With Jesus supporting our faltering knees, I pray that we will stand in embrace of our LGBTQ brothers and sisters and that we will stand in embrace of all people of good will, and of any faith, who seek to know the God of love and also seek God's peace. I believe we will. Whatever tomorrow brings, we will face it, with God's help, together.

"I Am Watching," Says the Lord

FEBRUARY 4, 2017

IN JANUARY 2017, President Donald Trump issued an executive order rescinding most federal funding from municipalities designated "sanctuary cities" for supporting undocumented immigrants. The President also issued a second executive order, by which he intended to initiate the building of a wall along the U.S. border with Mexico. Concurrently at the state level, the Texas State Senate considered Senate Bill 4, which required all local law enforcement officers to act as de facto *federal immigration agents and exposed municipalities that refuse to comply to legal sanctions. Senate Bill 4 was eventually signed into law in May 2017 by Texas Governor Greg Abbot.*

We are experiencing a time of rancor and division in our nation unseen in generations. Even people of faith and goodwill are conflicted, and, admittedly, Holy Scripture often offers counsel in more than one direction. On at least one issue, however, the witness of Holy Scripture is consistent and unequivocal: The treatment of immigrants and refugees.

Early in the Old Testament, God reminds the people of Israel of their own formative experience as immigrants and refugees in Egypt and of the suffering they received at Pharaoh's hand. God delivered the Israelites into the Promised Land, and God commands them to redeem their worst experience by embracing those in similar circumstances: "When an alien resides with you in your land, you shall not oppress the alien. The alien who resides with you shall be to you as the citizen among you; you shall love the alien as yourself, for you were aliens in the land of Egypt."[1]

God's people were human, as we are all human, and they often failed to follow God's command to offer sanctuary to aliens in their land. They were faithful to come together and worship together, proclaiming loudly, "This is the house of the Lord!" but they neglected God's call for grace toward immigrants and refugees. The prophet Jeremiah reminded the people that worship is pleasing to God only as an outgrowth of empathy and justice. And in what does God's justice consist? Through Jeremiah, God says: "If you truly amend your ways and your doings, if you truly act justly one with another, if you do not oppress the alien, the orphan, and the widow, or shed innocent blood in this place, and if you do not go after other gods to your own hurt, then I will dwell with you in this place." And God ends this injunction ominously: "I am watching, says the Lord."[2]

Jesus himself likewise commands his followers to care for the vulnerable. In the Parable of the Good Samaritan,[3] Jesus gives us the model for how to care for the sojourner in need. In Matthew 25, Jesus proclaims that those who welcome the stranger in their midst actually welcome Jesus himself and have a place in God's kingdom, while those who do not will be cast out. And the author of the Letter to the Hebrews makes the point most eloquently, "Show hospitality to the stranger, for by so doing some have entertained angels unaware."[4]

Finally, the Book of Ruth chronicles the story of the widowed Moabite Ruth, an immigrant who moves to Israel with her mother-in-law Naomi. Ruth offers a poignant speech of loyalty and commitment to her mother-in-law and her newly adopted country. In later centuries, rabbis constructed a Jewish catechism from Ruth's speech.[5] In other words, Ruth the immigrant became the very model for what it meant to be a faithful Jew. Just so, we—who are ourselves a nation of immigrants—can learn lessons of fortitude and faith from today's immigrants and refugees who seek shelter in our great land. Like Ruth and like our forbearers, they hope for a new life of safety and prosperity for their families. Like Ruth and like our forbearers, they wish to work hard and contribute to our communities. They can remind us of our best selves, but first we must receive them with grace and compassion.

On Civil War Monuments

AUGUST 13, 2017

ON JULY 10, 2015, *the Confederate battle flag was removed from the South Carolina Capitol Building. The removal was endorsed by Governor Nikki Haley and other state leaders after the flag was used as a symbol of white nationalism by Emanuel AME Church mass shooter Dylann Roof. The flag's removal encouraged debate across Southern states about the enduring presence of Civil War symbols and monuments. This debate crescendoed on August 12, 2017, when white nationalists converged on Charlottesville, Virginia to protest the removal of a Robert E. Lee statue. The vast majority of people, including those who cherish Southern heritage, were appalled by the events in Charlottesville. Many sought a way both to condemn the legacy of racism and to remember that which is redeemable about Southern history. This essay is my contribution to that conversation.*

Slavery is the blight of American history. It is irredeemable, and no mitigating factor can dilute its scourge. In any discussion of the antebellum South or the Civil War, slavery must have a central voice, because it was a central cause of the war. A review of the several Southern states that issued "Declarations of Causes" to accompany their acts of secession makes this clear.[1]

The declarations focus much on economics, but the economics are thoroughly and explicitly undergirded by slavery. The declarations of Mississippi and Texas are the most forthright in their admission that secession intended to preserve and perpetuate slavery. The Mississippi declaration crescendos, "Our position is thoroughly identified with the institution of slavery—the greatest material interest of the world." The Texas declaration says, "[In 1845, Texas] was received as a commonwealth [by the United States] holding, maintaining and protecting the institution known as negro slavery—the servitude of the African to the white race within her limits—a relation that had existed from the first settlement of her wilderness by the white race, and which her people intended should exist in all future time."

Whatever other contributing factors to which one may point with regard to the Civil War, the war was certainly about slavery; and as the first nation in the history of the world founded on the premise that "all men are created equal and endowed by their Creator with certain unalienable rights," we continue to struggle with its blight.

The Contemporary Struggle

As I write, that struggle manifests itself in conversations about the removal of Confederate-related statues across the South. Some of these statues are of Southern generals such as Robert E. Lee. Others are memorials to Confederate soldiers who died in the war. In virtually every instance, the argument over whether statues should go or stay is fraught with urgency and emotion. In my own city of Houston in recent weeks, the furor has overflowed to envelop statues of such figures as Christopher Columbus, who died a century and a half prior to the Civil War, and Sam Houston, who vehemently opposed secession, spoke in favor of the gradual elimination of slavery, and was the nineteenth century's greatest advocate of Native American rights. Regardless of one's point of view regarding Civil War monuments, making weighty decisions in the heat of emotion almost always leads to unintended consequences. In the hope of contributing a tempered perspective, I offer the following.

Why did they fight?

My son is named for my great-great-great-grandfather, Ira Griffin Killough. Killough moved to LaGrange in Fayette County, Texas, in 1851 from Bolivar, Tennessee. He married a Texan woman, became a landowner and a farmer, and established a hard but prosperous life.

Before the war, Ira Griffin Killough owned no slaves. During the war, he served in the Confederate Army and took up arms against the United States. After the war, he served in the Texas legislature; and, in 1876, he traveled north of the Mason-Dixon Line to attend the Philadelphia

World's Fair, where Alexander Graham Bell introduced the telephone. His life begs the question: Why did he fight?

In 1860, seventy percent of Southern Americans did not own slaves.[2] Why did any of them fight?

Part of the answer is that, despite not owning slaves, Southern soldiers fought to perpetuate the Southern way of life, which was borne on the backs of slaves. Even for non-slave owners, slave society was, in the words of author Gordon Rhea, the Southerner's "foundation experience":

> More than 4 million enslaved human beings lived in the south, and they touched every aspect of the region's social, political, and economic life. Slaves did not just work on plantations. In cities such as Charleston, they cleaned the streets, toiled as bricklayers, carpenters, blacksmiths, bakers, and laborers. They worked as dockhands and stevedores, grew and sold produce, purchased goods and carted them back to their masters' homes where they cooked the meals, cleaned, raised the children, and tended to the daily chores. "Charleston looks more like a Negro country than a country settled by white people," a visitor remarked.[3]

It is also worth noting, however, that in the first half of the nineteenth century, a time exceedingly different from our own, citizens identified much more closely with their various states than with the nation. Life was locality, and "the United States" was, for many, much more abstract than Texas, Fayette County, or LaGrange. Indeed, to an extent it was Abraham Lincoln's soaring wartime rhetoric that birthed the conception of the nation that we hold dear today.

To read such a conception backward into the antebellum worldview—especially in the South—is an anachronism. Only if we remember and grasp this can we understand a primary motivation for war of the majority of the Southern rank and file and, indeed, very many Southern officers: They fought to defend their homes—their states, their counties, their hometowns—from invading armies. Acknowledging this historic fact does not excuse slavery. Memorials to those who died, in the communities from which they hailed and for which they often gave their lives, is common among both victors and vanquished in war.[4] This long-standing and common tradition ought, perhaps, to affect our consideration of some Southern Civil War memorials.

Memorials to the Common Soldier

And yet, there is an additional critical, complicating factor: The vast majority of Confederate monuments trace to the era of Jim Crow, the period after the end of Reconstruction and the passing of *Plessy v. Ferguson* in 1896 until the 1920s.[5] Jim Crow laws were Southern state and local governments' *de jure* method of enforcing an underclass existence upon black Americans. Hand-in-hand with Jim Crow, communities across the South erected monuments to the "Lost Cause" as an emotional and psychological reminder to both white and black Americans of who was superior and who was inferior. Some of these monuments were statues of Southern military leaders on horseback, while others were of common soldiers.

The plaques on such monuments often include a simple dedicatory phrase, along with the date of installation, but when one digs into the origin of particular monuments, the intention behind their erection is revealed. The statue known as "Silent Sam" on the University of North Carolina campus is a good example. Silent Sam is a statue of a common soldier, installed on June 2, 1913, and the dedication speech was delivered by North Carolina industrialist and former Confederate soldier Julian Carr.[6]

Carr's speech is long and florid,[7] and he does, indeed, honor the memory of the common soldier. Yet, as he warms to his subject, Carr refers to the Daughters of the Confederacy, who paid for Silent Sam, and says, "God bless the noble women of my dear Southland, who are today as thoroughly convinced of the justice of [the Southern] cause." He then defines that cause:

> The present generation, I am persuaded, scarcely takes note of what the Confederate soldier meant to the welfare of the Anglo Saxon race during the four years immediately succeeding the war, when the facts are, that their courage and steadfastness saved the very life of the Anglo Saxon race in the South—When "the bottom rail was on top" all over the Southern states, and today, as a consequence the purest strain of the Anglo Saxon is to be found in the 13 Southern States—Praise God.

Carr immediately follows his homage to the Anglo Saxon race with a personal story that reinforces for both the white and black communities the penalty for a black person forgetting her place, a place of which the memorial itself serves as a visual reminder:

> I trust I may be pardoned for one allusion, howbeit it is rather personal. One hundred yards from where we stand, less than ninety days perhaps after my return from Appomattox, I horse-whipped a negro wench until her skirts hung in shreds, because upon the streets of this quiet village she had publicly insulted and maligned a Southern lady, and then rushed for protection to these University buildings where was stationed a garrison of 100 Federal soldiers. I performed the pleasing duty in the immediate presence of the entire garrison...

So which aspect prevails in our consideration: The raising of a memorial to the common soldier, or the original intent of that memorial as a tool of societal oppression?

Memorials to Generals

Beyond monuments dedicated to common soldiers, we must also consider statues to Civil War leaders. There are more Southern statues to Robert E. Lee than any other Civil War figure. Who was Lee? He was a reluctant rebel who, like the soldiers who served under him, most closely identified with the state from which he hailed. Lee wrote to his sister on the eve of the war, "With all my devotion to the Union and the feeling of loyalty and duty of an American citizen, I have not been able to make up my mind to raise my hand against my relatives, my children, my home."[8]

After the war, Lee strove to reestablish the bonds of union. Lee wrote to Virginia Governor John Letcher,

> The duty of its citizens, then, appears to me too plain to admit of doubt. All should unite in honest efforts to obliterate the effects of the war and to restore the blessing of peace. They should remain, if possible, in the country; promote harmony and good feeling, qualify themselves to vote and elect to the State and general legislatures wise and patriotic men, who will devote their abilities to the interests of the country and the healing of all dissensions. I have invariably recommended this course since the cessation of hostilities, and have endeavored to practice it myself.[9]

In addition to his words, Lee dedicated the remaining years of his life in contribution to the commonweal, most notably serving as president of Washington College. He became a lay leader in his church and even paid the minister's salary when collections proved insufficient.[10]

Robert E. Lee, like other Southern planters, owned slaves. He took up arms against the United States. He also fought to defend his home state. And at war's end, he became a laudable, and even extraordinary, citizen. Again we must ask, which aspects of Lee's history prevail in our consideration?[11]

A Way Forward

I offer this: The National Park Service preserves and operates more than seventy parks related to the Civil War, many of these on the sites of Civil War battles. During my childhood, my family visited many such parks, from Shiloh to Gettysburg. The Civil War parks are equal parts solemn and educational. At both the pristine Union cemeteries and the cannonball-marked Confederate mass graves, there is an air of introspection and prayer. In these places, even a century and a half after the war, the sense of grievous loss to our nation, and of the tragedy of brother killing brother, is palpable. These parks are our great national memorials to Civil War dead, both Northern and Southern. They should continue to be such, and they should be treated as hallowed ground. As education laboratories, they are also the most appropriate places for Civil War generals to have prominence, with the focus on military strategy and tactics.

With regard to Civil War monuments in other public spaces, the time period in which they were erected, and the intention for their construction—often explicit and recorded—should be complicating factors. It is unreasonable, and perhaps unthinkable, to ask black Americans to acquiesce to the continued presence on public ground, i.e. spaces that belong equally to all Americans, of monuments that honor the very people who fought for the overarching cause of keeping black Americans' ancestors in bondage and that were erected a half-century later with the intention of declaring to black Americans that they are an underclass.

In the case of Civil War monuments that do not embody these complicating factors, Confederate monuments should at very least be supplemented, side-by-side, with monuments to those who lived and died under the scourge of slavery, those who championed the freedom and rights of black Americans, and those who risked their lives helping slaves escape to freedom. If there is, indeed, a pantheon of Southern heroes, surely members of these three categories deserve the places of greatest honor.

If, in the end, we are to look retrospectively to Robert E. Lee, perhaps we should evaluate Southern monuments taking our cues from the General himself. When asked his opinion about the creation of memorials to the war, Lee said in 1869, "I think it wiser…not to keep open the sores of war but to…obliterate the marks of civil strife, to commit to oblivion the feelings engendered."[12]

It may be that only then can the specter of our national blight be exorcised.

Afterword

DURING HOLY EUCHARIST in the medieval church, rather than sitting stationary in pews, congregants milled around the nave. Sanctus bells were rung during the Eucharistic Prayer to draw the attention of worshipers at those moments when Christ was believed to enter the bread and wine. When the bells rang, the holiest moment of the Eucharist had arrived. The bells signaled that God was present in the midst of the people.

At Christ Church Cathedral in downtown Houston, the mighty bell in our bell tower tolls every hour. Whether I'm working in my office, praying in the church, or walking downtown, I can hear the crystal-clear peal on the air. Our church bell—like Sanctus bells in a medieval church—signals the presence of God in the midst the city.

Christ Church Cathedral sits just a few blocks away from both City Hall and St. Joseph's Hospital. Nearer still are the JP Morgan Chase Tower, the courthouses, a federal prison, and Minute Maid Park, where the world-champion Astros play. The Cathedral exists in the very midst of the commercial, recreational, governmental, legal, and health-care center of Houston. When the Cathedral bell tolls each hour of every day, it serves to remind the entire city that God is present not only in our Sunday worship but also in the midst of each of these parts of our lives. God's politics bears upon how we do business, how we treat our citizens, and how we care for those who are hurting. The Gospel lays claim to the entirety of us.

Without this recognition, our faith becomes akin to the gauzy and placid portraits of Jesus that dot Sunday School rooms in churches across the South, the religious version of a Thomas Kinkade painting: sweet, comforting, and vaguely nostalgic, but powerless to transform lives, much less the world.

God is in the midst of the city, and the Gospel proclaims an alternative vision for the world. It is exactly in times of disaster, danger, and political turmoil that God's politics is the most vitally important. As the Body of Christ, with the Gospel in one hand and the newspaper in the other, we are called to center ourselves in God and then proclaim the Gospel, with the clarity and strength of that mighty Cathedral bell.

Endnotes

Introduction - God's Politics
1. The depiction of Palm Sunday that follows comes from Marcus J. Borg and John Dominic Crossan, *The Last Week: The Day-by-Day Account of Jesus's Final Week in Jerusalem* (San Francisco: HarperCollins, 2006), 1-30.
2. Zechariah 9:9-10.
3. John Howard Yoder, "The Bible and Civil Turmoil," in *For the Nations: Essays Public and Evangelical* (Grand Rapids, MI: Eerdmans, 1997), 84.
4. Andrew C. Doyle, *The Jesus Heist: Recovering the Gospel from the Church* (New York: Church Publishing, 2017), 98-100.
5. Ibid, 101.
6. Ibid, 101-102.
7. Karl Barth, "Barth in Retirement," *Time Magazine*, May 31, 1963, accessed March 19, 2018, http://content.time.com/time/subscriber/article/0,33009,896838,00.html.

Look for the Helpers
1. Farmer, Patricia Adams, "The Quaking and Breaking of Everything," *The Jay McDaniel Blog*, accessed April 21, 2013, http://www.jesusjazzbuddhism.org/boston-the-beautiful-finding-faith-after-the-quaking.html.
2. Maura Judkis, "Mr. Rogers and Newton: Quote and image goes viral," *The Washington Post*, December 17, 2012, accessed April 21, 2013, http://www.washingtonpost.com/blogs/arts-post/post/mister-rogers-and-newtown-quote-and-image-goes-viral/2012/12/17/a462f598-485c-11e2-820e-17eefac2f939_blog.html.
3. Steve Garnaas-Holmes, "Marathon kindness," *Unfolding Light Blog*, accessed April 21, 2013, https://www.unfoldinglight.net/reflections/1868.
4. Frederick Buechner, *Beyond Words: Daily Readings in the ABC's of Faith* (San Francisco: HarperCollins, 2004).

Paris, Syria, and Christ the King
1. 1 Kings 1:1
2. Liz Sly, "Syria is emptying," *Washington Post*, September 14, 2015, accessed November 22, 2015, https://www.washingtonpost.com/world/syria-is-emptying/2015/09/14/2b457a86-534f-11e5-b225-90edbd49f362_story.html.
3. Paul Goldsmith, "Why Paris shows that ISIS are losing and we who maintain the 'greyzone' are winning," *Goldblog*, November 14, 2015, accessed November 22, 2015, http://pjgoldsmith.com/2015/11/14/why-paris-shows-that-isis-are-losing-and-we-who-maintain-the-greyzone-are-winning/.
4. Luke 10:25-37.

5 Rev. Tommy Williams, Sr. Pastor at St. Paul's United Methodist Church in Houston, pastors' op-ed for *The Houston Chronicle.*

Skimming the Headlines

1 Elizabeth Bromstein, "Scientists say giant asteroid could hit earth next week, causing mass devastation," *Yackler Magazine,* July 9, 2016, accessed July 17, 2016, http://yackler.ca/blog/2016/07/09/scientists-say-giant-asteroid-hit-earth-next-week-causing-mass-devastation/.

2 Colossians 1:16-20.

9/11, Fifteen Years Later

1 David Stout, "Flight 93 Tape is Played at Terror Trial," *The New York Times,* April 12, 2006, as posted on *Neil Mishalov's Web Site,* accessed September 11, 2016, http://www.mishalov.com/wtc-flight-93-transcript.html.

2 Williams, Rowan, *Writing in the Dust: After September 11* (Grand Rapids, MI: Eerdmans, 2002), 3.

3 Maria Hinojosa, 'On September 11, final words of love," *CNN.com./U.S.,* September 10, 2002, accessed September 11, 2016, http://archives.cnn.com/2002/US/09/03/ar911.phone.calls/.

4 Williams, *Writing in the Dust,* 5, 3.

The Election, God, and Our Bliss

1 Pew Research Center, "3. Voters' evaluations of the campaign," last updated November 21, 2016, accessed March 19, 2018, http://www.people-press.org/2016/11/21/voters-evaluations-of-the-campaign/.

2 Philippians 4:7.

3 Jonah 2.

4 Nouwen, Henri J.M., *Ministry and Spirituality* (New York: Continuum, 1996), 246.

The Mystic Chords: Post-Election Thoughts

1 John Cassidy, "Closing Arguments: The Logic of Negative Campaigning," *The New Yorker,* November 5, 2016, accessed November 6, 2016, https://www.newyorker.com/news/john-cassidy/closing-arguments-the-logic-of-negative-campaigning.

2 Lizzie Deardon, "Donald Trump's victory followed by wave of hate crime attacks against minorities across US - led by his supporters," *Independent Daily Edition,* November 10, 2016, accessed November 13, 2016, http://www.independent.co.uk/news/world/americas/us-elections/donald-trump-president-supporters-attack-muslims-hijab-hispanics-lgbt-hate-crime-wave-us-election-a7410166.html.

3 *CBS News,* "You voted Trump" yelled at man while he's beaten in Chicago streets," last updated November 12, 2016, accessed November 13, 2016, http://www.cbsnews.com/news/you-voted-donald-trump-yelled-man-beaten-chicago-streets/.

4 Camila Flamiano Domonoske, "Anti-Trump Protest In Portland, Ore., Turns Destructive, Declared A Riot," *NPR News,* November 11, 2016, accessed November 13, 2016, http://www.npr.org/sections/thetwo-way/2016/11/11/501685976/anti-trump-protest-in-portland-ore-turns-destructive-declared-a-riot.

5 Abraham Lincoln, "First Inaugural Address, March 4, 1861," *Bartley.com,* accessed November 13, 2016, http://www.bartleby.com/124/pres31.html.

6 The Very Reverend Barkley Thompson, "Thinking about death," *God In The Midst Of The City Blog,* October 23, 2016, https://rectorspage.wordpress.com/2016/10/23/thinking-about-death/.

7 The Very Reverend Barkley Thompson, "The election, God, and our bliss," *God In The Midst Of The City Blog,* November 6, 2016, https://rectorspage.wordpress.com/2016/11/06/the-election-god-and-our-bliss/.

8 Riaz Patel, "What a Gay, Muslim, Pakistani-American Immigrant Learned Traveling to Rural Alaska the Week Before the Election," *Glenn Beck Blog,* November 10, 2016, accessed November 13, 2016, http://www.glennbeck.com/2016/11/10/what-a-gay-muslim-pakistani-american-immigrant-learned-traveling-to-rural-alaska-the-week-before-the-election-2/?utm_source=glennbeck&utm_medium=contentcopy_link.

7 O'Clock News

1 Luke 1:30.

2 cf. Mark 4:40, Mark 5:36, John 14:27, etc.

All Israel Will Be Saved

1 Michael Wolffsohn, *Eternal Guilt?: Forty Years of German-Jewish-Israeli Relations* (New York: Columbia University Press, 1993), 194.

2 This crucial point is often lost because of a common, poor translation of Romans 3:22, "the righteousness of God through faith in Jesus Christ for all who believe." A more accurate rendering of the Greek is "the righteousness of God through the faith of Jesus Christ for all who believe."

3 Romans 9:30-32.

4 Romans 11:25-26.

"I Will Send You": In the wake of Hurricane Harvey

1 *World Vision,* "Hurricane Harvey: Facts, FAQs, and how to help," accessed September 3, 2017, https://www.worldvision.org/disaster-relief-news-stories/hurricane-harvey-facts#damage

2 Abby Hamblin, "Exactly how much rain Harvey has brought to Houston, elsewhere in Texas," *The San Diego Tribune,* August 29, 2017, accessed August 13, 2017, http://www.sandiegouniontribune.com/opinion/the-conversation/sd-how-much-rain-has-houston-texas-gotten-20170829-htmlstory.html.

3 Christ Church Cathedral would ultimately receive more than $250,000 in hurricane relief funds from churches and individuals across the country.

The Ten Commandments

1 Bob Allen, "Baptist Congressman Can't Name Ten Commandments," *EthicsDaily.com,* June 22, 2006, accessed March 4, 2018, http://www.ethicsdaily.com/baptist-congressman-cant-name-ten-commandments-cms-7527.

2 Ibid.

3 Walter Brueggemann, "The Book of Exodus," in *The New Interpreter's Bible* (Nashville: Abingdon Press, 1994), 1:849.

Without Love, All Is Lost

1. Gary Olson, "Why So Little Empathy and Compassion Within American Culture?" *Common Dreams*, January 14, 2019, accessed April 16, 2018, https://www.commondreams.org/views/2018/01/14/why-so-little-empathy-and-compassion-within-american-culture.

2. Ibid.

3. Peter Bazalgette, "As a society, are we losing our empathy?" *The Irish Times*, January 30, 2017, accessed August 16, 2018, https://www.irishtimes.com/culture/books/as-a-society-are-we-losing-our-empathy-1.294792.

4. Gary Olson, "Why So Little Empathy and Compassion Within American Culture?" *Common Dreams*, January 14, 2019, accessed April 16, 2018, https://www.commondreams.org/views/2018/01/14/why-so-little-empathy-and-compassion-within-american-culture.

5. Harper Lee, *To Kill A Mockingbird* (New York: Grand Central Publishing, 1960), 39.

6. 1 John 4:8.

7. David Noise, "Beware America's Shocking Loss of Empathy," March 6, 2016, accessed August 16, 2018, https://www.psychologytoday.com/us/blog/our-humanity-naturally/201603/beware-americas-shocking-loss-empathy.

8. Mark, Sullivan, *Beneath a Scarlet Sky* (Seattle: Lake Union Publishing), 102.

9. 1 John 3:14.

Liberty, Christian and American

1. William Sloane Coffin, *The Heart is a Little to the Left: Essays on Public Morality* (New Hampshire: University Press of New England, 1999), 77.

2. Ibid.

Birth: A Reflection for Independence Day

1. Abraham Lincoln, "Annual Message to Congress –Concluding Remarks," quoted on *Abraham Lincoln Online*, from *Collected Works of Abraham Lincoln*. Edited by Roy P. Basler, et al. 2006, accessed July 2, 2017, http://www.abrahamlincolnonline.org/lincoln/speeches/congress.htm.

I Own Guns, and I Believe in Gun Control

1. Michael S. Schmidt, *"F.B.I. Confirms a Sharp Rise in Mass Shootings Since 2000,"* The New York Times, September 24, 2014, accessed August 29, 2015, https://www.nytimes.com/2014/09/25/us/25shooters.html.

2. Nicholas Kristof, "Kristof: Lessons From the Virginia Shooting," *New York Times*, August 25, 2016, accessed August 29, 2015, https://www.nytimes.com/2015/08/27/opinion/lessons-from-the-murders-of-tv-journalists-in-the-virginia-shooting.html?smid=fb-share&_r=2.

3. Mark Moe, "A grammar lesson for gun nuts: Second Amendment does not guarantee gun right," *The Denver Post The Idea Log for Opinion*, February 12, 2013, accessed August 29, 2015, http://blogs.denverpost.com/opinion/2013/02/12/a-grammar-lesson-for-gun-nuts-second-amendment-does-not-guarantee-gun-rights/33796/.

4. Jeffrey Goldberg, "The Case for More Guns (and More Gun Control)," *The Atlantic*, December 2012 Issue, accessed August 29, 2015, https://www.theatlantic.com/magazine/archive/2012/12/the-case-for-more-guns-and-more-gun-control/309161/.

5. Isaiah 2:4

"I Am Watching," Says the Lord

[1] Leviticus 19:33-34
[2] Jeremiah 7:5-7,11
[3] Luke 10:25-37
[4] Hebrews 13:2
[5] Ruth 1:16-17

On Civil War Monuments

[1] "The Declaration of Causes of Seceding States: Primary Sources, Georgia," *Civil War Trust website,* accessed August 13, 2017.

[2] "Selected Statistics on Slavery in the United States," *Civil War Causes.org.,* accessed August 13, 2017, http://www.civilwarcauses.org/stat.htm.

[3] Gordon Rhea, "Why Non-Slaveholding Southerners Fought: Address to the Charleston Library Society, January 25, 2011", *Civil War Trust website,* accessed August 13, 2017.

[4] In June 2017, I traveled to Germany. In the city of Worms, in a public park, I was surprised to find an enormous World War I statue memorializing local German soldiers who died in that horrific conflict. On one level, the First World War was history's greatest folly to chauvinistic pride and military aggression, and in it the German Army utilized weapons so egregious that they were subsequently universally banned. I had not expected to see any German war monument from either world war. On another level, World War I included millions of young German men who fought and died to defend hearth and home. They served bravely for a local cause—the defense of their home communities such as Worms—which was itself subservient to a sinful cause, the aggression of the German Empire. I considered the memorial with detachment, since the First World War is a century past and I have no familial or cultural relationship to anyone who died in it, and I walked away from the monument concluding that yes, a monument to the local fallen is an appropriate expression of the community's loss and that no, it does not excuse the sin of German militarism.

[5] "Whose Heritage? Public Symbols of the Confederacy," *Southern Poverty Law Center,* last modified April 21, 2016, accessed August 13, 2017, https://www.splcenter.org/20160421/whose-heritage-public-symbols-confederacy.

[6] Julian S. Carr, "Unveiling of Confederate Monument at University. June 2, 1913" in the *Julian Shakespeare Carr Papers #141, Southern Historical Collection,* The Wilson Library, University of North Carolina at Chapel Hill. http://hgreen.people.ua.edu/transcription-carr-speech.html.

[7] The Rev. Greg Jones pointed me to the Silent Sam monument. Greg also gave me the description of Carr's speech as "florid."

[8] *The American Civil War Website,* Civil War Quotes, General Robert E. Lee, accessed August 13, 2017, *http://www.brotherswar.com/Civil_War_Quotes_4b.htm.*

[9] Ibid.

[10] Michelle Boorstein, "This is the church where Robert E. Lee declared himself a sinner. Should it keep his name?" *The Washington Post,* August 22, 2017, accessed August 13, 2017, https://www.washingtonpost.com/news/acts-of-faith/wp/2017/08/22/this-is-the-church-where-robert-e-lee-declared-himself-a-sinner-should-it-keep-his-name/?utm_term=.03b7fd323858.

[11] Occasionally, the question arises with regard to the appropriateness of monuments, school names, street names, etc., honoring other American historic figures, such as the Founding Fathers. Considering the sum total of a figure's life seems to me a good means for evaluating these cases, too. In my opinion, outside of Civil War figures, the contributions to our nation and world by most other figures in our national pantheon almost always outweighs those figures' vices, especially when their vices are pervasive of their historic context (such as racial attitudes). Judging past historic characters solely by our contemporary moral standards is fraught with pitfalls.

[12] Lisa Desjardins, "Robert E. Lee opposed Confederate monuments," *PBS NewsHour,* August 15, 2017, accessed August 13, 2017, http://www.pbs.org/newshour/updates/robert-e-lee-opposed-confederate-monuments/.

Acknowledgements

THIS BOOK IS DEDICATED to the people of Christ Church Cathedral. For almost 180 years, Christ Church has proclaimed God in the midst of the city and remained committed to God's politics in downtown Houston. It is a privilege to serve among such faithful people. The final stages of this book were completed during a sabbatical from Christ Church, and I am grateful both to the Cathedral and the Diocese of Texas for the time away. I am indebted to the Honorable Linnet Deily, friend and parishioner, for providing the foreword. The Rev. Dr. Steve Wells of Second Main Baptist Church and the Rev. Tommy Williams of St. Paul's United Methodist Church, both in Houston, have become important friends and colleagues, and their voices informed a number of the pieces included in this book. Thanks also to my extraordinary editor, Lucy Chambers, Fiona Bills and Marla Garcia at Bright Sky Publishing, and my assistant Louise Langford, who brought my endnotes into good Kate Turabian style. Of course, my love and gratitude toward Jill, Griffin, and Eliza is limitless. I am especially grateful to Jill for her willingness to let me slip away for a day or two of writing here and there at Mourning Dove, our little place in the country where God's presence is always palpable. Finally, I wish to thank my parents, Charlotte and Robert Thompson. When I was a child, Mom made sure I was in Sunday school every week, and it was there that I first heard the life-transforming words of the Gospel. And though we may not always agree politically, it was Dad who taught me to pick up the paper, watch the news, and think with depth and care. For their love and nurture, I am grateful.

About the Author

BARKLEY THOMPSON is the dean of Christ Church Cathedral, in Houston, Texas, a historic, downtown congregation of 3,000 members. Christ Church has a more than century-long legacy of ministry to the marginalized and operates The Beacon, Houston's largest day center for the homeless. He is the author of the book *Elements of Grace,* as well as numerous journal and magazine articles. He also writes the popular blog *God in the Midst of the City.* Barkley holds degrees from Hendrix College, the University of Chicago, and the Seminary of the Southwest in Austin, Texas. He is married to Jill, and they have two children.